UNFAITHFUL

REBUILDING
TRUST AFTER
INFIDELITY

UNFAITHFUL

REBUILDING
TRUST AFTER
INFIDELITY

GARY & MONA SHRIVER

LIFE JOURNEY®
Bringing Home the Message for Life

COOK COMMUNICATIONS MINISTRIES
Colorado Springs, Colorado • Paris, Ontario
KINGSWAY COMMUNICATIONS LTD
Eastbourne, England

Life Journey® is an imprint of
Cook Communications Ministries, Colorado Springs, CO 80918
Cook Communications, Paris, Ontario
Kingsway Communications, Eastbourne, England

UNFAITHFUL
© 2005 by Gary Shriver and Mona Shriver

First printing 2005
Printed in the United States of America

3 4 5 6 7 8 9 10

Cover Design: Image Studios/Rob Huff

Unless otherwise indicated, Scripture quotations are taken from the
HOLY BIBLE, NEW INTERNATIONAL VERSION®. Copyright © 1973,
1978, 1984 International Bible Society. Used by permission of Zondervan.
All rights reserved. Scripture quotations marked NASB are taken from the
NEW AMERICAN STANDARD BIBLE®, copyright © 1960, 1962, 1963,
1968, 1971, 1972, 1973, 1975, 1977, 1995 by The Lockman Foundation.
Used by permission. Italics in Scripture quotations have been placed by
the author for emphasis.

Library of Congress Cataloging-in-Publication Data

Shriver, Gary.
  Unfaithful : rebuilding trust after infidelity / Gary and Mona Shriver.
    p. cm.
  ISBN 978-0-7814-4268-8
  1. Adultery. 2. Spouses--Religious life. 3. Marriage--Religious
aspects--Christianity. 4. Shriver, Gary--Marriage. 5. Shriver,
Mona--Marriage. I. Shriver, Mona. II. Title.
BV4627.A3S57 2005
248.8'44--dc22
                              2005017936

CONTENTS

ACKNOWLEDGMENTS

We must first acknowledge a God whose love for us is greater than all our sin—our Lord who provides the hope and healing we human beings are so in need of. May we be his good and faithful servants.

To our counselor and brother, Sherman Glenn. Your guidance kept us on the path of healing. You not only heard our cries but also facilitated the forming of a ministry we so desperately needed ourselves. We are humbled by the trust you placed in us as you allowed us to come alongside other couples.

To Mike and Jo, who walked with us and were so instrumental in the development of the support group ministry. We would never have chosen this path to a friendship, but your validation, willing hearts, and encouragement so beautifully illustrate Romans 8:28. We can only pray the four of us will continue in ministry together for many more years.

To our prayer team. You are faithful members of the body of Christ. Some of you upheld us in the early days of our own crisis, and some came later as God led. We do not underestimate your value. God alone knows the work you have done for us personally and for the ministry we are privileged to be a part of.

To the couples who have participated with us in our Hope and Healing support groups. Your courage and strength are to be admired—you did not take the easy path. Thank you for opening yourselves up to us and for the many lessons you have taught us.

To Mary McNeil, our editor, who sat on a bench with us at Mount Hermon and believed our message was worth hearing. We believe God chose you to do the editing, and every reader will be blessed by the improvements you made in our manuscript. Those readers will never know what you did, but we do. It has been a privilege.

FOREWORD

In an age where marriage scandal is blared from every newspaper and TV set, Christians are strangely silent about their scandals.

In an age where vulnerability is the mark of the times, Christians are *not* vulnerable.

In an age where divorce is the common answer to adultery, Christians must declare, "There *can* be hope and healing!" In *Unfaithful,* Mona and Gary Shriver shout, *There is hope! Healing can come to your marriage!*

With gut-wrenching honesty, Mona and Gary open the most painful portion of their lives to you—the part labeled "Betrayal." No candy-coated answers are given. Pain, heartache, hopelessness, anger, and exhaustion all march across these pages. No simplistic answers are offered. Mona and Gary never say working through the horror of adultery is easy. What they do offer you is one couple's journey beginning with the revelation of betrayal through every stage of healing. You will discover how Mona and Gary found strength to endure the pain, how they learned to honestly acknowledge their losses, wrestle through forgiveness, and finally build hedges around their renewed relationship.

If you are walking through the pain of unfaithfulness, buy this book. If a friend is in the agony of betrayal, buy this book for him or her. We promise you will be lifted on wings of hope to the Healer and given practical help that can bring healing. We highly recommend this book!

DR. JOSEPH AND LINDA DILLOW
DR. PETER AND LORRAINE PINTUS
Authors of
Intimacy Ignited and *Intimate Issues*

INTRODUCTION:
Revelation

He reveals the deep things of darkness
and brings deep shadows into the light.
JOB 12:22

GARY'S STORY

It must have been about 9:30 as I pulled into the driveway. Everything looked dark and settled down for the evening. As I stopped the car, my heart pounded in my chest like never before. For a moment I wondered if I might be having a heart attack. I took a deep breath, got out of the car, and headed for the back door. I unlocked it and walked onto the back porch. I was right; everything was settled for the night. The three boys were in bed. The house was quiet. The only light was a dim glow from the master bedroom at the end of the hall. I made my way to our bedroom.

Our bedroom. I wondered if that would be the case in the aftermath of the bomb I was about to drop. I stopped and asked myself, *Should I really go through with this?* This could be the end of everything I know as my life: my family, my church, my business, my friends. Not one area of my life would be unaffected by the event about to occur. Should I

> **I STOPPED AND ASKED MYSELF, *SHOULD I REALLY GO THROUGH WITH THIS?* THIS COULD BE THE END OF EVERYTHING I KNOW AS MY LIFE: MY FAMILY, MY CHURCH, MY BUSINESS, MY FRIENDS.**

tell her or just keep living the lie?

No, I couldn't continue deceiving her. I had just spent the last two hours in my senior pastor's office confessing my sin. I confessed the double life I had been living for the last few years. I couldn't believe his first response. "Are you serious?" he asked. "I can never tell when you're kidding me. Are you really serious?" I sat in his office with tears streaming down my face, and he asked if I was serious. I just nodded, and he finally realized I *was* serious. Very serious. We talked and prayed, and he just kept looking at me. I knew what was going through his mind. He was saying great words of spiritual wisdom and offering words of encouragement, but behind his words, shock and disbelief were apparent. He referred to spiritual leaders who had fallen. He said, "This is happening all around us." At that point, I could only think, *That doesn't make this any less ugly.* I knew he was trying to encourage and comfort me in my darkest hour, but the darkness that enveloped me was beyond penetration. He and I both knew that everything was not all right and that it wasn't going to be all right.

He asked if Mona knew. I shook my head no. He looked me straight in the eye and asked, "Do you intend to tell her?"

I nodded.

"When?"

"Right now," I said. "I need to go right now."

It had taken all I could muster to meet my pastor and confess my dark and horrible behavior. I had to complete my confession. And I had to do it now. On my way home I thought of other men I knew who had committed adultery and didn't say a thing to their wives. They seemed to have gotten away with it. But a Bible verse kept ringing in my ears: "You may be sure that your sin will find you out" (Numbers 32:23).

And that it had. Earlier that afternoon the engineer at my office had confronted me with this "problem" he thought I had. He came quoting Matthew 18:15–17, saying that if I didn't come clean, he would go to my pastor with what he believed to be the "affair" I was having.

Affair. What a fluffy word. It sounds so cheery and acceptable. Lets call it what it really is. *Adultery!* Black hearted, not caring anything about anybody else, completely self-centered, the absolute epitome of

> ♥ ♥
>
> LET'S CALL IT WHAT IT REALLY IS. *ADULTERY!* BLACK HEARTED, NOT CARING ANYTHING ABOUT ANYBODY ELSE, COMPLETELY SELF-CENTERED, THE ABSOLUTE EPITOME OF SELFISHNESS.

selfishness. Adultery. And I was an adulterer. Finally after years of my wrestling with him, God had brought me to a point of brokenness. I just couldn't go on like this anymore. I had to tell Mona. The only way I could ever hope to save my marriage was to be totally honest. God was chasing me. I had to deal with it now!

I walked into the bedroom. The lamp on her bedside table glowed. There she lay, leaning back on her pillow propped up against the wall, reading something. She looked up and said, "How was your meeting?" Just about then our eyes met. "Honey? What's wrong?"

"I'VE BETRAYED YOU,"

I WHISPERED.

I hadn't rehearsed anything. I didn't know what to say. I just sat down on the bed next to her and looked at her.

"You're scaring me," she said.

I started to cry.

"Now you're really scaring me."

"I've betrayed you," I whispered.

Her eyes glazed over. She seemed to stare through me. "What?"

"I've been unfaithful to you," I repeated.

She went limp. I thought for a second she was going to pass out. Her stare went from distant to direct and cold.

"With who?" she demanded.

I said the name.

"I knew it," she said.

But I knew she didn't. I tried to hold her. She started to

hold me but then pushed me away. She was shell shocked.

"How long?" she asked.

I whispered, "A long time."

"How long?"

"A couple of years."

"Years? Ever since you started working with her?"

"Almost."

Her lip quivered.

As her world crumbled around her feet, my heart raced again. This

NO MORE LIES. NO MORE SECRETS. I HAD TO TELL HER EVERYTHING.

time I could feel it in my temples. How could I say more? *How can I, Lord? I can't tell her everything.* Yet God was insistent: *Tell her!*

I felt like Moses must have. *I can't, Lord. I can't!*

Tell her now! God demanded.

I had to tell her everything. God burned into my heart that if our marriage were to have any chance at all, it had to be with a clean slate. No more lies. No more secrets. I had to tell her everything.

"There's more."

"More? What do you mean more?"

"There was a one-night stand with another woman."

I honestly did think she was going to pass out at that point. Her eyes rolled back into her head, and then things got eerie.

After a long moment, she said, "We need to talk. But not here."

She asked me to leave the room so she could change

clothes. I knew at that moment our lives had changed forever, and I didn't know what to expect in the aftermath of my horrible revelation.

We didn't speak a word on that drive to our office. We got there, made coffee, and settled in the conference room. After we sat for what seemed to be an eternity, her blank stare suddenly focused, and the flurry of questions began. "Do you love her?"

"No, I love you."

"Do you want a divorce?"

"No, I want to stay with you. Do you want a divorce?"

"I don't know what I want. Why did you do this?"

I didn't know how to answer that question. I didn't know how I'd gotten where I was. I explained there had been no pursuit. I said that it was a friendship that had gotten out of control, and that I had felt trapped. I had never stopped loving Mona.

The blank stare was back. I kept trying to explain. She didn't want to hear—or couldn't hear—anything more. After a while she started asking me about the other woman.

EVEN IF WE HATED EACH OTHER AT MOMENTS, WE NEEDED TO HOLD ON, OR THIS MARRIAGE WOULD NOT SURVIVE.

"It was a one-night thing. Honestly, she threw herself at me. She made up her mind to have me. She set her sights, and she was going to have her way."

What was I saying? It was

all the truth, but what was I trying to do here? Justify my adultery? My *second* case of adultery at that!

I shut my mouth and started to cry again. I didn't know what to do. She didn't want to talk about it anymore. She didn't want anything from me. I was dying inside. I needed to know what she was thinking. She was in shock. Was she thinking of leaving? Was she going to ask me to leave? What was going on in her head?

My God, what have I done? In a matter of seconds I have ripped the heart from the woman I love.

I felt strongly about holding on to each other—not necessarily physically, but holding on to each other emotionally to keep Satan from driving a wedge any deeper between us. I knew in my heart of hearts, if we were to make it, we would have to do it together. We would have to hold on to each other and not let go. Even if we hated each other at moments, we needed to hold on, or this marriage would not survive.

It seemed there was nothing more to say. So we went home. I offered to sleep on the couch, but she declined my offer. She explained that if we were going to try to work this through, she saw no sense in my sleeping on the couch.

If. Such a small word to hold one's whole future.

It was quiet and still, but I knew the explosion was yet to come. She stared blankly into the corner of the ceiling. I lay there, knowing her mind was whirling. I was sure her thoughts were bouncing from one horrific scenario to another, and all I could do was lie next to her and watch as her entire foundation cracked, crumbled, and fell away. Every now and then a tear would roll down her cheek and a sob would escape her throat.

My God, what have I done? In a matter of seconds I have ripped the heart from the woman I love. The bride of my youth. Will she ever forgive me? *Can* she ever forgive me? I had no idea how much pain this would cause. If we make it through this, one thing is certain: we will never be the same again.

God, please forgive me.

Mona, if you can find it in your heart, please try to forgive me.

Mona's Story

I don't remember what book I was reading, but I do remember I never finished it. I threw it away. It would always remind me of that night.

I heard the back door open and thought, *Gary's home a little early—must have been a short meeting.*

I heard him walk down the hallway. He opened the bedroom door and just stood there, staring at me.

I said something like, "How'd your meeting go?" I watched as my husband of more than nineteen years began to crumble. His body sagged as if under a heavy weight.

His eyes filled with tears and he said, "We have to talk."

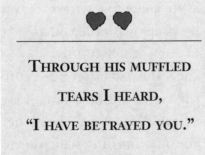

THROUGH HIS MUFFLED TEARS I HEARD, "I HAVE BETRAYED YOU."

I knew something was terribly wrong and remember thinking someone had died. *I wonder if it's our pastor? He must have found out something horrible at the meeting.* Compassion overwhelmed my heart, and I reached out my arms, inviting him in. "Oh honey, what's wrong?"

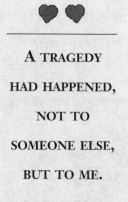

He came to the bed, sat down by me, and allowed me to hold him while sobs racked his body. I had never seen him like this. Through his muffled tears I heard, "I have betrayed you."

A TRAGEDY HAD HAPPENED, NOT TO SOMEONE ELSE, BUT TO ME.

I felt my body stiffen. A tragedy had happened, not to someone else, but to me. My mind refused to process his words. "What?"

"I have been having an affair."

These words penetrated, and I felt my own tears rise. I heard the word come from my mouth before I realized I had even thought it: "Who?" Why was there no surprise when he said her name? I remember even then knowing there was really only one true possibility. I also remember other names going through my head, almost hoping he'd say one of those instead. I had never suspected. I trusted them both implicitly. He was my husband whom I loved and who I thought loved me. She was his coworker, a fellow church member, and the woman I had considered my best "Christian" friend for the past three or four years.

"How long?" I asked.

"A while," he mumbled.

I began to feel the first stirring of rage. *"How long?"*

"A couple of years maybe."

Not just once or even twice. Not a few weeks or even a few months! Was I a complete idiot? How could something like this go on for so long and I not even have a clue? They must have thought I was so stupid! How many times had they laughed at my naïveté?

I pulled away from him, unable to touch him, unable to do much more than breathe.

Then I heard these words: "There's more."

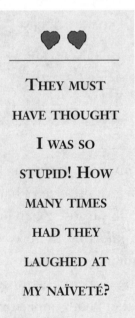

THEY MUST HAVE THOUGHT I WAS SO STUPID! HOW MANY TIMES HAD THEY LAUGHED AT MY NAÏVETÉ?

More? More than the destruction of my life, my family, my church, my home? *More?*

"I also had a one-night stand with another woman." Then he named her, a twenty-year-old single mother and non-Christian with whom we'd had business dealings.

"She came over one night uninvited when you were gone."

Here? In my house? The office had been attached to our home up until about a year ago. Nothing was sacred. Every aspect of my life was involved. My home. The church where I always sat with my best friend. Our office. Even the hospital where I worked as a nurse was filled with people who crossed over into these aspects of my life.

I was nauseous. I was repulsed. This was something

horrible men did. Not my Gary! Not the man I had always jokingly said I'd have to catch in bed naked before I'd ever believe he'd be unfaithful. The man couldn't lie for beans.

Gary was not the man I had thought he was, but I was no longer sure who I was, either. For that matter, who were we as a couple? *Were we a couple?*

"We have to talk," I said, "and not here." I wanted to protect my children. I didn't want them to know we were dying.

We only had one place to go. I got out of bed to get dressed. I looked at him and froze. This was the man I'd

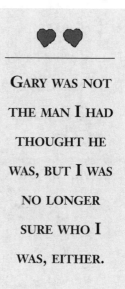

GARY WAS NOT THE MAN I HAD THOUGHT HE WAS, BUT I WAS NO LONGER SURE WHO I WAS, EITHER.

been married to for almost twenty years. He'd been my lover, my best friend, and my confidant. My family loved him because he was so wonderful. All my friends thought he was wonderful—he did dishes, laundry, and changed diapers. I had lost count of how many times I'd been told how lucky I was.

I could not bear to have him in the room, and I asked him to leave so I could get dressed. It seemed unnatural to change clothes in front of him now. My body was numb, wooden, overwhelmed. The weight Gary had walked into our bedroom wearing was now being shared.

I woke our oldest son and told him we had to go to the office for a while. He sleepily mumbled an answer, and we left. We made the short ride in silence. A barrier lay

♥ ♥

A BARRIER LAY BETWEEN US THAT NEITHER OF US COULD CROSS—OR MAYBE WE DIDN'T WANT TO.

between us that neither of us could cross—or maybe we didn't want to.

When we arrived at the office, I made coffee. We sat at our lunch table, and I asked questions. "Do you love her?"

"No."

"Do you want a divorce?"

"No."

"Does her husband know?"

"I think she's waiting to see if I really tell you first."

"You have to let her go."

"I know."

The particulars of our conversation blur in retrospect. He told me he had gone to the church to confess to our pastor. The pastor had called in another pastor, they had all prayed, and then they sent Gary home to tell me.

He told me that our engineer had confronted him that day. He had suspected what was going on and had gone to his pastor, who advised him to confront Gary. What strength that must have taken for such a young man!

Gary said God had been preparing him for this revelation for a long time. Promise Keepers, meetings, sermons, his conscience. He had felt trapped in the relationship with his coworker for quite a while. If he broke it off, he knew the ramifications and the possibility of losing his family, his business, and his church. They had broken it off many times in the past and yet would find themselves back together. He couldn't remember when it started, but the last time they'd been together had been just three days earlier.

As I tried to pin down the time period of the affair, it became clearer that it had been going on for about three years. It began shortly after she started working with us. Her marriage was in trouble and had been for a very long time. She talked about it often. She and I had talked about it often together. I felt like such a fool. Gary and I had even discussed her vulnerability and her attractiveness before they started working together. I knew she envied our relationship, but I hadn't realized that she had actually been wishing for Gary himself. She, as it turned out, knew better than I what my marriage was really like. He said neither one of them had pursued the other.

THAT NIGHT MY LIFE TOOK ON A NEW TIMETABLE: BEFORE THE AFFAIR, DURING THE AFFAIR, AND AFTER THE AFFAIR.

That night my life took on a new timetable: before the affair, during the affair, and after the affair. Everything during was now marred and distorted. Our family trip to Disneyland, Gary and I going to Hawaii. I recalled snippets of conversation with both Gary and my friend and suddenly heard and saw completely different things.

He asked me that night if I would come to work for him full time and we'd rebuild our lives and the business. I was furious. How dare he! I told him I wasn't going to give up any more of me than he'd already ripped away. I was a

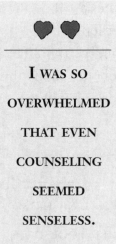

I WAS SO OVERWHELMED THAT EVEN COUNSELING SEEMED SENSELESS.

nurse. I was a good nurse. I couldn't lose that, too.

He asked me if I wanted a divorce, and I said no. What would that do to our boys? Where would I go? What would I do?

We talked about counseling. To what end? I was so overwhelmed that even counseling seemed senseless.

Gary told me about the night the young woman had come over and seduced him. He said it was very intentional on her part. I said that did not exonerate him. He knew that. The story of that one-night stand sounded like a despicable movie. I knew at that very moment that God had allowed the seduction for one purpose—so Gary could see how deep into sin he was. Now Gary could see the man he had become. Having an affair with someone you care about and someone who cares about you can take on the appearance of romance. This one-night stand could only be seen for what it was—a leap into the filthy recesses of sin.

Soon it seemed there was nothing left to talk about. Or maybe it was just that we were incapable of talking anymore. Gary reassured me that he loved me and wished he could take it all away. He asked for my forgiveness and told me he'd do anything I asked. I knew that adultery was biblical grounds for divorce, but I didn't know if that applied when the offender repents and asks for forgiveness.

My mind, soul, and body were exhausted by the events of the night. I knew I wanted to follow God in this, no matter where that led. I knew I needed a godly friend and felt again the pain of loss. Who would I call now that my two best friends had betrayed me?

When we arrived home, Gary asked if I wanted him to sleep somewhere else. I said no. I figured he'd been in my bed during the last three years, what difference would it make now?

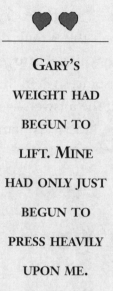

GARY'S WEIGHT HAD BEGUN TO LIFT. MINE HAD ONLY JUST BEGUN TO PRESS HEAVILY UPON ME.

And so I clung to my edge of the bed and listened to my husband fall into a deep and restful sleep. Sleep would evade me. I would spend most of what was left of that night in the family room crying.

Gary's weight had begun to lift. Mine had only just begun to press heavily upon me.

THE STORY OF REVELATION

That night was more than ten years ago. We can now say with absolute sincerity that we have fully healed from the adultery. Our marriage is strong and mutually satisfying. We have love and trust.

We refuse, however, to say that our marriage is better. We had heard "now they have a better marriage" in reference to couples who had gone through serious problems, and it only had caused us more pain. We'd thought our marriage was good before the adultery. We loved each other; we were best friends. Certainly we had issues; all couples do.

But our marriage prior to the adultery had value and was good. What happened to us happened to a good marriage. Most people have a hard time believing that because if they do, it makes every marriage vulnerable. So many of those who think they have a "good marriage" think they're safe from this destroyer of marriages. Certainly there are those instances when the whys and wherefores are clear, but often all the answers we seek cannot be found. So instead we say we are wiser than we were then. We make better choices now. And we no longer believe we are invulnerable to attack.

MARRIAGES CAN HEAL. WE KNOW, BECAUSE OURS DID.

If you have picked up this book, you are probably going through, or love someone going through, the aftermath of finding out about a spouse's adultery. Our hearts break for you, and we want you to know there is hope. Marriages can heal. We know, because ours did. We know, because we've been able to support other couples facing this anguish. We also know it will be one of the hardest things you will ever go through. It would have been far easier *at the time* for us to split up. And we would not have been condemned for doing so. That same thing is true for many others.

We know these words seem hard to believe. When you go through this crisis, you feel as if the weight of the world is pressing down on you. Then the fiery darts from hell come faster and faster, and your shield of faith seems to offer little protection. You are fighting for your marriage with every ounce of strength you can muster until you begin to fear you're going to lose the battle. Remember, this is where Satan wants you, and he will be faithful to keep the burners on high. Why? He wants nothing more than to see your marriage fail. He wants you to become another statistic. So let us repeat ourselves: You don't have to give up! You can make it!

How? We want to share with you what made the difference. We were Christians when the adultery happened. We are still Christians. What we will share with you is definitely from a Christian perspective, but it is also from a practical, real-life perspective.

Is our marriage now perfect? No. We still have issues, and we've learned that some will remain until we get to heaven. Perhaps we've learned to pick our battles with more grace and wisdom. We have also learned that some battles were due to our own selfish desires and far removed from the marriage partnership.

We are not, nor do we claim to be, experts in anything. We have no educational or professional background to validate us. Those people are out there, and their resources are available to you. You'll need them, too. But if you seek two ordinary believers to share their extraordinary experience, then here we are. We do not undertake this task lightly. This is not our idea of fun. In the early stages of writing, our emotions often overwhelmed us, and there were times we would leave our desks sobbing. We found ourselves crying over things we hadn't cried over in years. Our God, however, is a great God and gracious to his people. In time we felt that we were merely observing a sad story, rather than reliving the awful past.

When we were in the deepest pit of our crisis, we wanted more than anything to know a real-live, normal couple whose marriage had survived this horror. We needed someone who could look us straight in the eye and say, "You guys can do this! It won't be easy, but you can do it." We needed people like us who had continued living, working, and parenting throughout their ordeal. We asked our pastor and our Christian counselor. We sought such people and never found them.

What did evolve from our experience was a support group called "Hope and Healing," supervised by our Christian counselor. Over the last few years, as we have ministered to couples going through the pain of adultery recovery, we have heard a lot of the same themes. One is the desperate need to connect with another couple who has survived, and the inability to find this resource. Another is the common dynamic that seems to run through the experience. Often we were there to simply reassure couples they were not going crazy, but experiencing a horrendous crisis. These are some of the things we'll be sharing with you.

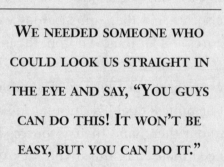

WE NEEDED SOMEONE WHO COULD LOOK US STRAIGHT IN THE EYE AND SAY, "YOU GUYS CAN DO THIS! IT WON'T BE EASY, BUT YOU CAN DO IT."

We can relate only our experience. Yours will be entirely

different, but we are certain that you, like the couples in our groups, will find some value in the sharing. Seek other godly counsel, and ask God himself to help you filter through and apply what is right for your situation. We highly recommend the book *Torn Asunder: Recovering from Extramarital Affairs* by Dave Carder with Duncan Jaenicke (Moody, 1995). We'll define some terms by borrowing from the cast of characters of *Torn Asunder*.

- ◄ Infidel: the one who strays and gets involved in an illicit relationship
- ◄ Spouse: the one married to the infidel
- ◄ Partner: the person with whom the infidel was involved

Obviously, one can play any of these roles.

When we refer to *revelation*, we are talking about the event where the infidel admits to the spouse that an illicit relationship has occurred. The illicit relationship will be referred to as an "affair" with the disclaimer that the word sounds much too playful for the seriousness of this offense—much like calling a murder an "accident." It is a commonly accepted and understood term, however, so we will use it.

We also need to acknowledge one last term that defies

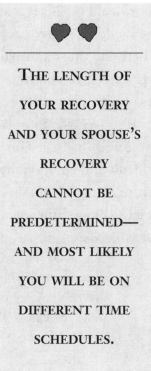

THE LENGTH OF YOUR RECOVERY AND YOUR SPOUSE'S RECOVERY CANNOT BE PREDETERMINED—AND MOST LIKELY YOU WILL BE ON DIFFERENT TIME SCHEDULES.

definition: time. You will read over and over again that healing took "time." We all want to know just how long that time is. We have sat across from couples weary from the effort and battle, tears streaming down their faces, saying, "It's been (insert specific time here). Isn't that long enough?" The answer is "apparently not." The length of your recovery and your spouse's recovery cannot be predetermined—and most likely you will be on different time schedules.

The realization that we were "fully healed" came as a surprise—a surprise that it had happened some time before. We encourage you to give up any timetable you may have in your brain; it will only frustrate you and be detrimental to your healing. This is a marathon, not a sprint, a journey with many stops. Enjoy each small victory. Take a short holiday when you must and when you can. As long as either of you has a need to continue working, it's not over. We can only encourage you with the fact that it is worth the journey.

How we wish we could sit across a table from you and share face-to-face. Our Hope and Healing groups, although difficult and emotionally draining, have been the most fulfilling ministry of our lives. We have seen the Lord do marvelous things, and we will pray those same marvelous things for you.

> ... who comforts us in all our troubles, so that we can comfort those in any trouble with the comfort we ourselves have received from God. For just as the sufferings of Christ flow over into our lives, so also through Christ our comfort overflows.
>
> —2 Corinthians 1:4–5

COMMITMENT

Commit your way to the Lord;
trust in him and he will do this:
He will make your righteousness shine like the dawn,
the justice of your cause like the noonday sun.

PSALM 37:5–6

MONA'S STORY

(Less than six months after revelation)

My parents were not happy in their marriage. Quite frankly, I don't know if they ever were. I do remember a brief time when I was ten that seemed to be happy. It was right after a move. Dad had a good job, Mom was able to stay home, and we lived in a nice house in a nice area. Soon, however, things reverted to what was normal for us—Dad too sick to work, Mom working, and another move into a less nice house. Still, I had that brief glimpse of what I thought was a normal home where everyone liked each other. I wanted that for myself when I grew up and had my own home.

When things went well with my family, we went to church. When they did not, we did not. Attendance seemed to be associated with our circumstances and not with our desire to worship God. The church we would attend was legalistic; entrance to heaven was determined by how well you obeyed the rules. By the time I was a teenager, I knew I couldn't obey all the rules. I was going to hell and therefore determined to have fun here on earth while I could. I rejected the church, God, and anything or anybody religious. However, the childish prayer of a young girl stayed with me. *Please, God, let me have a happy marriage.*

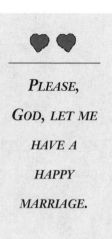

PLEASE, GOD, LET ME HAVE A HAPPY MARRIAGE.

That prayer seemed to be answered when Gary and I married in May of 1974. I was twenty and he was twenty-one. Neither one of us was a believer. He hadn't been raised in any church or religion. We both had left home at eighteen. We both had worked since we were young, and we both were pretty responsible.

In 1979 a friend of Gary's came to see him. He shared his story of recent salvation and faith, and before he left, he gave Gary a Bible and "prayed the prayer" with him. When I got home, Gary informed me of what had happened. I scoffed. *He just doesn't know what this is all about like I do,* I thought. I'm sure my negative expression and body language clearly said that this was a subject we were not going to discuss. Gary wisely made no changes in our lifestyle. He did begin to read that Bible, although he had no follow-up or formal disciple-ship opportunities. On the rare occasion when the subject of faith came up, I would again scoff and tell him he was going to hell right along with me for all the things he continued to do—like smoking, drinking, and cussing. Satan had also been faithful to provide us with another friend who thought the same way I did. Gary didn't argue much; he would just look at us and say that wasn't what he was reading in the Bible.

Time went on, and God pursued me. He used many things over the next three years to soften my heart and expose my need. Finally, in 1982 I determined to read the Bible for myself and resolve this issue once and for all. I started in Matthew and read straight through. By the time I got to Romans 7, I said yes to God's truth. However, with very little reverence, I announced to him that he was going to have to prove it to me. He did then. He still does today.

Seven years later I was feeling a spiritual hunger not yet satisfied. I began an inductive Bible study, and my whole life changed. I saw truth. I learned I could understand truth and discern error. I had run from a God I'd been told about, not from a God I knew.

The peace and the freedom were exciting.

The understanding that I would be accountable for what I knew was frightening.

The desire to continue learning was like nothing I'd ever experienced. So God took those next few years and taught me. During that process, I made a commitment to him. I would never leave or run again, no matter what. That com-mitment has been tested with some painful difficulties, but it has held fast.

I tell you all this to help you understand what a big part this played in my response to Gary's adultery. God had taught me truth—his truth. I had chosen to believe and obey, and I knew that my obedience would often be the opposite of what I felt like doing. It did not make what Gary and I went through any easier, but I really felt I had no choice other than to walk through it. I simply did not have release from my heavenly Father to seriously consider divorce. It wasn't an option. We had three young children who would either benefit by our ability to recover or pay dearly if we split up. That's the spiritual reason. The other reasons are not so spiritual.

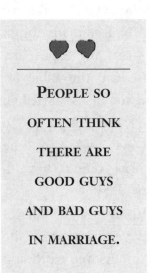

PEOPLE SO OFTEN THINK THERE ARE GOOD GUYS AND BAD GUYS IN MARRIAGE.

First, there was pride. I was proud of my happy marriage. I knew so many who did not have a happy marriage, and I had been fortunate to have one. In fact, I knew of only one other couple that liked each other as well as Gary and I, and who were as compatible as we were. We often discussed it. There was no way I was going to throw that all away. I valued it. And Gary seemed to want to rebuild it. Therefore, I would try.

Second, there was more pride. People so often think there are good guys and bad guys in marriage. It's easy to observe couples, watch the dynamics, and get a glimpse of who's the easier one to live with. I've already told you my family loved Gary. Gary was easygoing and fun, loving, talented, a giver by nature. Remember, he was the one husband who helped around the house and with the kids. Most of the wives were jealous, and most of the men gave him a bad time for making them look bad. Who do you think most people thought was the "better one"? Even under the circumstances of adultery, when it was all said and done, I knew that most would end up "understanding" him.

Third, I really didn't have anywhere else to go. I had never been as close in spirit with anyone else as I was with my husband. That "good marriage" had provided me with an intimate partner, one I took all my troubles to, a friend I could go to with anything and he would still love me and help me through it. I was going through hell. I knew it wasn't going to be over quickly. I had a choice: I could go through it alone, or I could go through it with Gary.

I HAD A CHOICE: I COULD GO THROUGH IT ALONE, OR I COULD GO THROUGH IT WITH GARY.

I was sitting on the couch after another day of pain. Endless pain. All-consuming pain. I was tired of hiding my pain from the world. On the days I worked at the hospital, it took every-thing I had just to make it through my shift without breaking down. One of the girls had walked into the break room when I was there and, looking straight at me, said, "You look like you just lost your best friend." I wanted to scream at her that I had in fact lost both of them, but I mumbled something benign instead and left the room. I was checking and rechecking every medication I gave, every order I completed. My mind was not working right. For the first time in my life, I experienced stress so severe it was incapacitating. I didn't know how much more I could take.

And there were the boys. Our oldest was withdrawing more and more. Our middle son was getting into more and more trouble. And who had time for the youngest? I was not only a failure as a wife, but a blatant failure as a mother, too. I knew Gary was tired, too, but this wasn't my fault. I didn't do this. He did it.

I heard Gary come in, and I heard the boys greet their father. Normal sounds. But this wasn't a normal household. Nothing was normal anymore. I wasn't normal. All I could do was cry and ask questions. I was obsessed. Everyone would be fine if I could just move on. They could all just live their normal little lives with all the other normal people.

ALL I COULD DO WAS CRY AND ASK QUESTIONS.

I grabbed my car keys and ran out the door. I got in my van and just drove. I had to get away. I had to go. Tears ran down my face. Was I ever going to be able to stop crying? I couldn't remember the last day I didn't cry. Was there never to be any relief from this hell? I screamed at God, *When is this going to be over? Is it ever going to be over? How could you allow this? Why didn't you protect us from this? Why? Why? Why?*

I didn't know where I was going. *I'm not even safe driving. Oh, God, just kill me and end this, please!* The name of a friend popped into my head, and I turned the car toward her house. About halfway there I thought of her husband and children. How could I go there and expose them to this? They didn't even know about it.

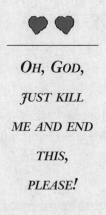

OH, GOD, JUST KILL ME AND END THIS, PLEASE!

Another friend. She knew. I could go there. I turned in the opposite direction. She, too, had children. I couldn't go there. Her husband was a friend of Gary's. I couldn't do this to them.

I turned again. Where can I go? *Maybe a bar. I'll go to a bar. I'll get drunk and stay in a motel. Maybe I'll even pick up a man and see what it's like to commit adultery.* Even as I thought these things, I knew I couldn't go. I'd end up sick, or worse, I'd drive drunk and kill somebody else. Besides if I committed adultery, we'd have to go through all the AIDS testing again, and I couldn't do that. A book I'd read said you should get tested after adultery. We discounted it at first, but when we stopped to consider the possibilities of whom Gary had been exposed to, it was frightening. And so we had gone and gotten Gary tested—one of life's most embarrassing moments. Filling out forms with questions such as, "How many sexual partners have you had in the last six months?" Knowing the tech who comes to draw your blood has read the answers. Then waiting for days, weeks. One night I dreamed the test came back positive, and then I was positive, and we had to tell the partner and her husband, and they were positive, and we were all dying and everyone knew why. At least that part was a nightmare from which I could wake up.

I drove aimlessly, going down lists of names in my mind. Who could I go to? Who would comfort me?

I thought of another friend, this one without children. I could go there. They would love me. Then I remembered they weren't Christians, and God had impressed on me that those who would help me had to be Christians. *You need Christians right now.*

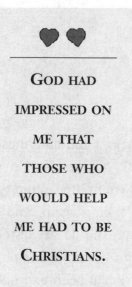

GOD HAD IMPRESSED ON ME THAT THOSE WHO WOULD HELP ME HAD TO BE CHRISTIANS.

I stopped my van at the top of an overpass. I laid my head on the steering wheel and sobbed like a baby. There was no one. No one. No one I could lay this burden on and not be sorry later that I had done so. There was only one person who could truly help me and who needed to experience this with me. My husband.

As I turned the van to go home, I spoke again to God. *You're not going to let me go anywhere else, are you?* I had committed to him and to Gary. One way or another the three of us would see this thing through.

GARY'S STORY

(Less than six months after revelation)

I can honestly say that I always felt committed to Mona. "Yeah, right," you say. "Even during the affair?" I know it sounds weird, but I felt committed.

I had been surrounded by solid marriages all my life. I was

raised in a small middle-class community in northern California. If ever there was a "Beaver Cleaver" existence, I was raised in the midst of it. My folks were happy. I can't remember a fight or a harsh word between them. My grandparents were very much a part of our lives, and they always seemed more than happy. I wasn't raised in a Christian home, but morals and a sense of right and wrong were a part of my upbringing. I was brought up to believe that marriage was for life. It was something of value.

We didn't go to church very often during my childhood. I knew there was a God, and I had heard of Jesus his Son, but I really didn't know anything about a relationship with him.

As I left my teens and entered my twenties, I started to feel a tug on my heart. I really didn't know what to do about it, but there was a definite void. When I was in my late twenties, a fellow musician I had lost contact with for a couple of years called one day. He had been writing songs and had heard I had a recording studio; he would love to drive down and show me his work and maybe record a demo. A few days later, he was knocking on my door, ready to share these songs he had written about Jesus, his new personal Savior. I had known this guy well when we played in a band together, and he was no Christian. As a matter of fact, he was quite the opposite. But this guy had really changed. He was much softer spoken and not nearly as pushy. He didn't use profanity once while we were together, and that was not like him at all. He shared his songs and his heart, and it wasn't more than a couple of sessions later I found myself praying with him the prayer of salvation.

So what's this all have to do with Mona and my commitment to our marriage?

I never really thought I was a prime candidate for adultery. I was committed to our marriage, and I didn't think I was what you would call "high risk." So how did I get there?

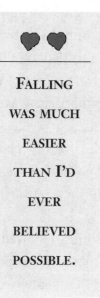

FALLING WAS MUCH EASIER THAN I'D EVER BELIEVED POSSIBLE.

The best description I ever heard was "baby steps." I let myself get into a position of innocent intimacy with another female. Our conversations were innocent enough—family, friends, and ministry. But one baby step led to another and to another, and before I could turn and run, I was in way too deep. Falling was much easier than I'd ever believed possible. And at that point in our marriage, I was angry with Mona for putting me on the back burner of her priorities. I could point to many reasons why I could be angry with her, but the bottom line is that I felt she didn't want me in any way at all.

But she was my wife. I loved her. I had made a commitment to her before God when we said our marriage vows. "I'm in for life," I always said. But adultery changed things. When God brought me to that point of brokenness and it was time to get this all out in the open, I felt a sense of commitment that I knew could only come from God. I would use all my strength to convince Mona I was here to stay, and nothing she could do or say would change that. And boy, did I find out that she could do and say plenty! It had to be God's strength that fashioned in me what I called "armadillo skin." She used words I had never heard her say before. But I was committed.

After a few months on this plane, I found out what commitment was all about. I had started out with a purposed and diligent attitude. I was there at all hours—and I mean all hours—with answers to her questions. I talked and explained until I ran out of words. And then I got mad.

Here we go again, I thought. I was angry and tired. It wasn't going like I'd thought it would. I'd figured if I could just get right with God and confess my sin, he would reward me with a healing process. I had sinned, yes, but I had also obeyed and dealt with the sin honestly—with God and with Mona and with my church.

I HAD SINNED, YES, BUT I HAD ALSO OBEYED AND DEALT WITH THE SIN HONESTLY—WITH GOD AND WITH MONA AND WITH MY CHURCH.

I had done everything the way I was supposed to, yet the situation just wouldn't get any better. I had expected a rocky road, but I hadn't expected the road to get steeper and more treacherous with time. It seemed the more I tried to smooth things over, the angrier Mona got. Her barrage of questions continued to increase, and my anger reached new depths. I had committed the sin, yes, but how much punishment was I supposed to take?

After a few months, the shock wore off for Mona. I think she honestly wanted to forgive me and keep the marriage going, but as she became convinced of my sincerity, she grew angrier and more demanding. She insisted that I spend every waking moment convincing her I was here for the duration, that I wasn't going to quit. And I had better answer every question exactly as I had answered that same question the last time and the time before and the time before. Any slight variance in my answer was cause for suspicion. Why had my answer changed? What wasn't I telling her? What lie had I just been caught in? It was an endless assault. *Is this the life, the wife, I can expect from here on out? Am I to never be more than her whipping boy?* It seemed the further we went into the supposed healing process, the further we went from a marriage partnership. I was beginning to lose hope. Quite frankly, if this was the way our lives were going to be, I wasn't interested.

So what's up with this, God? You brought me through for this? You've guided me—here? I've been faithful in every way since my confession. So where are you? Where is your mighty healing power? I thought you were on my side.

As I sat there screaming this prayer to God, I began to feel guilty. Who was I? The adulterer! The infidel! Who was I to think I deserved anything better? The issues that had brought Mona and me here were becoming more evident to me, and I was beginning to understand why couples didn't survive infidelity. I was questioning our survival for the first time. God's allowance of divorce for adultery was beginning to make sense. The wounds were so deep for both of us. The intense pain pushed me to think about self-preservation and less about "us" preservation. But through all this I knew in my spirit that God wanted us to survive; it was in his will for our marriage to make it. *But where are you, God? Where are you now?*

Then I heard his still, quiet voice say, *I'm right here. And, Gary, I'd rather have you right here, angry with me, than not here with me at all.*

Those few words spoke volumes to me, that picture of a loving Father wanting his angry son. How gracious he is. My anger didn't push him away. Our relationship meant more to him than how I was behaving at the moment or how I had behaved in the past. His was the ultimate example of commitment.

THE *AGAPE*, SELF-SACRIFICIAL LOVE THAT GOD HAS FOR ME WAS THE ONLY MODEL I COULD FOLLOW TO GET US THROUGH THIS CRISIS.

Within a few short moments, a rush of understanding flooded my mind and heart. Suddenly I saw the parallel of my relationship with God in my relationship with Mona. The *agape*, self-sacrificial love that God has for me was the only model I could follow to get us through this crisis. It wasn't going to come from me, but from him through me. The only thing I had to do was to stay committed to God, to Mona, and to our marriage recovery. *Not in my strength, Lord, but in yours.*

THE STORY ON COMMITMENT

So just what is commitment? The dictionary tells us it is "the act or process of entrusting—the act of doing." In the case of adultery recovery, it is primarily a decision to do everything within your power to heal your marriage. We made mistakes. We both struggled. We had difficulty with the entrusting and the doing. But we were committed, and eventually with God's help we processed through.

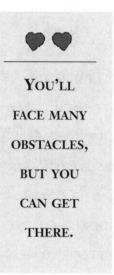

YOU'LL FACE MANY OBSTACLES, BUT YOU CAN GET THERE.

Even more important is to whom and what you commit. Some committed people have created big problems because they were committed to things that did not edify their marriage. An infidel committed to a partner and a spouse committed to payback are examples of commitments that cause more harm than healing. Even more deceptive and harmful is a commitment to making sure your spouse becomes the person you always wanted him or her to be.

We encourage you to consider and acknowledge just what it is you are committed to. This is a long and difficult journey. You'll face many obstacles, but you can get there. Commitment is one of the major tools you'll need.

COMMIT TO GOD

The primary commitment that will influence much of your behavior is commitment to God. In him we find the strength and the energy for this journey. To him we look for guidance for the doing, especially when our emotions are in such turmoil. In the midst of the worst times, all we could do was ask him to guide us, to reveal the next step we should take.

Mona, the fixer of this relationship, found she needed to wait for the Lord's guidance and refrain from acting on her own. Gary, the conflict-avoider, found he needed to act when the Lord did indeed guide him. Both of us found these roles difficult, but our motivation came from our commitment to God. We could do for him when we had no desire to do for ourselves individually, much less for each other.

We got so weary, feeling like we had done all we could do. We began to ask ourselves if maybe restoring our marriage was just too hard. Then the Lord would remind us that it was indeed too hard for us, but not for him. He would renew our strength and guide our path; he reminded us of who he was. Some days all we could do was cry out to him, but that was enough. He who created marriage is worthy of our commitment, and we can trust him. He is faithful.

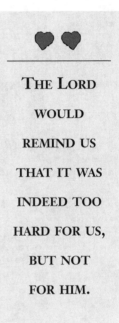

THE LORD WOULD REMIND US THAT IT WAS INDEED TOO HARD FOR US, BUT NOT FOR HIM.

If this sounds too simplistic, we suggest you sit at his feet in prayer, honestly state your feelings, and ask for his help. Then wait and see what he does.

COMMIT TO SELF

Second is a commitment to yourself that from this day forward you will focus on being the husband or wife God has called you to be. Decide that when you don't want to do what you know is right (and there will be plenty of those times), you will admit your feelings honestly to God and to yourself.

At times, we had no desire to be a godly spouse. We asked God to give us a heart that would honor him.

The infidel's commitment to be the spouse God has called him or her to be permanently seals the separation between infidel and partner. There can be absolutely no contact between them. When things get tough at home, and they most certainly will, Satan will be right there to tempt you to run back. Rejection of these desires is imperative and will be a vital part of your recovery. Denial that these desires exist will only increase your vulnerability and risk. Be honest with yourself and with God. Recognize the source of these desires is based on a lie. Focus on the commitment you've made that is based on truth.

> **THE REALITY IS THAT THE MARRIAGE NEEDS TO CHANGE, OR YOU WOULDN'T BE IN THE SPOT YOU'RE IN, AND THE ONLY ONE YOU CAN CHANGE IS YOU.**

For the spouse, this is an opportunity for prayer—like you need another one! But God calls us to pray for one another and gives us a specific prayer for this circumstance: "Therefore I will block her path with thornbushes; I will wall her in so that she cannot find her way" (Hosea 2:6). Pray that the way of sin would be difficult, that God would surround you and your mate with a hedge of protection.

We often had to battle feelings of "I was a good spouse"

or "I could be a much better spouse if he or she would ..." or "I have done enough." The reality is that the marriage needs to change, or you wouldn't be in the spot you're in, and the only one you can change is you. It doesn't mean you throw away what was good about you. It means that you commit to evaluate yourself honestly as the spouse God has called you to be.

However, you are not to measure yourself against whatever your spouse may have wanted you to be. Gary's partner wore high heels; Mona did not. During the early days of our recovery, we went shoe shopping together and bought a pair of white heels. They were attractive, and Mona wanted to be attractive to her husband, so she put them on. She wore them once; they killed her feet. In addition to that, the shoes became a visual reminder of the pitiful truth that she was competing with her husband's partner. She threw them away because they were far removed from what God had called her to be and were in fact a detriment to our recovery. This is a common scenario. Of course, it's not shoes for everyone. But the principle and the motivation behind the choice are the same. You are not committing to be the spouse some other person wishes you would be, only to fulfilling God's purpose for you and your marriage.

COMMIT TO YOUR SPOUSE

Last, commit to your spouse. Commit that you will do everything you can to establish an environment for healing. Commit to being honest from this point forward, which can be a difficult journey for some of us. It means acknowledging that dishonesty led you down your current path. It means admitting to your spouse that a healthy marriage requires trust and intimacy and that you are willing to cultivate those qualities in your relationship. And it means deciding that you will not be satisfied with anything less than full healing, no matter how long it takes. You must be willing to look at yourself honestly and be willing to change.

Some of you are probably sitting there saying, "Commit to my spouse? This is the person who just took a two-by-four to my marriage and my heart." We understand the emotions. Please note your commitment is not to overlook the past or pretend like nothing happened, but *to provide the environment for healing,* to be willing to work together for something worth saving.

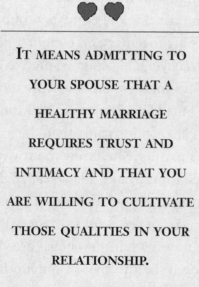

IT MEANS ADMITTING TO YOUR SPOUSE THAT A HEALTHY MARRIAGE REQUIRES TRUST AND INTIMACY AND THAT YOU ARE WILLING TO CULTIVATE THOSE QUALITIES IN YOUR RELATIONSHIP.

Gary said this very well. "I know what I'm asking. Every time you've fallen backward, I've caught you. But this time I let you fall on purpose. You hit hard, you were injured, and I just stood there. And now I come to you and say, 'It's okay, honey, just fall back and I'll catch you.'"

The desire to avoid being injured again is real. For Mona, it took time and many small tests to see if Gary really meant it. It took many hours of discussion and sharing of truth.

When she could not trust, she admitted it. Eventually she came to the point of acknowledging she could not, would not, live like this any longer. That left two choices: trust or leave. The commitments we've discussed eliminated one of those choices.

Gary sat through many hours of honest pain. He had to be willing to give Mona time, to endure the tests, and to pass them. And at the same time, he had to be willing to let God lead his spouse on her own journey of change.

Here is where the real commitment comes in. When you get through the hard part at the beginning of the rebuilding process, when your spouse begins to forgive, when you begin to relax—and God knows you both need to relax—there is a glimmer of light at the end of the tunnel. This is where you can make a critical and costly mistake. This is where you can really blow it.

How? Stop working on the marriage. Shut down. Determine you have done enough. Let us reassure you of the truth of the old saying, "It ain't over till it's over." Healing is a process, and in the situation of adultery, a tediously slow process. You each will process at your own pace. Remember, the infidel began this process before the affair even began. The spouse typically begins at revelation. Also, each of you will have separate personal issues in addition to your couple issues. If a

♥ ♥

COMMITMENT TO GOD, YOURSELF, AND YOUR SPOUSE— IN THAT ORDER—ENABLES THE PROCESS TO MOVE FORWARD.

healthy marriage is your goal, you must allow your mate to process through in God's time. It is worth it!

Commitment to God, yourself, and your spouse—in that order—enables the process to move forward. We realize that some will struggle with this order. Shouldn't self always be last? Isn't putting self above your mate one of the things that got you here? We are not recommending this for a lifestyle, only to help process through the adultery. Remember, your commitment to self is not for self-satisfaction. It is a commitment to, from this day forward, focus on being the wife or husband God has called you to be. Adultery is a train wreck. Each of you is severely damaged emotionally, spiritually, and physically. Healing that damage takes time.

Your number one commitment to God will remain unchanged. We are confident that as he heals you and your marriage, he will correct as he sees fit. We only know that if we had not focused on these three commitments, our marriage most likely would not have survived. We hated why we had to do this, and it was the hardest thing we ever did, but we are so glad we did it.

FAITH

Consequently, faith comes from hearing the message,
and the message is heard through the word of Christ.
ROMANS 10:17

GARY'S STORY

(Revelation day)

I wasn't stupid. I knew it was wrong. I knew what the Bible said about adultery. I'd read about times God had hardened hearts and left people to their own perversions—like Saul and the people described in Romans 1. I knew these things. So how could I, a Christian, be buried up to my eyebrows in sin? In adultery? Why couldn't I just stop?

Driving to work that Monday morning, I was again plagued with these same thoughts. Where was God? Why didn't he help me with this? I had been with her again last week. Then I'd spent the weekend racked with guilt and begging God for forgiveness. I had been in that place many times. I knew in my heart of hearts that the only way out was to do something drastic. I needed to cut off the sinful relationship and confess to my wife. God had been telling me that all along. He wouldn't leave me alone about it. But how could I do it? Owning up to my sin would affect not only my marriage, but also my entire family, my business, my church, my service for God, my public ministry. Nothing would be untouched, nothing untainted by my black-hearted behavior.

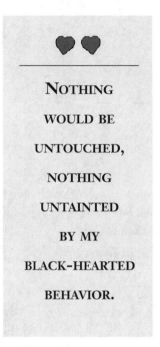

NOTHING WOULD BE UNTOUCHED, NOTHING UNTAINTED BY MY BLACK-HEARTED BEHAVIOR.

I hadn't gone looking for this. Neither had she. It just happened—two lonely people, two neglected spouses. No matter how I justified it, though, God kept bringing spiritual conviction to my secular lifestyle. Many times the pastor had said in his Sunday sermons, "My door is always open," and I knew God was talking to me. *Oh, God, forgive me. Help me! Give me the strength to stay away from her this time.*

As I pulled up into the office parking lot, the back door opened, and out walked my twenty-year-old engineer. He was an easygoing guy, talented, and doing well in the studio.

When I got out of the car, I noticed the look on his face. He didn't look happy. Great! Employee problems were all I needed right then. Didn't I have enough to deal with? *Thanks a lot, God. I pray to you for strength, and just where I need it the most, you turn up the heat.* I felt my heart race as we walked into the office. I needed some relief, not more pressure.

His greeting consisted of "We need to talk."

"Okay," I said. "Let's go into the studio." He led the way.

When he pulled the door closed behind him, I knew my instinct had been right. This was not going to be a good day. My anxiety level rose. Was he going to quit?

I could tell by the way he sat that he was nervous, uncomfortable.

"I come to you quoting Matthew 18:15–17. 'If your brother sins…, go and show him his fault.'"

I knew the passage. "If your brother sins against you, go and show him his fault, just between the two of you. If he listens to you, you have won your brother over. But if he will not listen, take one or two others along, so that 'every matter may be established by the testimony of two or three witnesses.' If he refuses to listen to them, tell it to the church; and if he refuses to listen even to the church, treat him as you would a pagan or a tax collector."

"Gary," he said, "I believe you are in sin. After wrestling with God for a while, I went to my pastor. He advised me to confront you with this. And so I am." He paused, sighing as if he'd just completed a very difficult task.

"What?" I exclaimed. "What makes you think that?"

What did he know? How could he know? She and I were good—as far as lying goes. We knew how to keep our affair discreet. We were careful around everybody, and especially around fellow workers. I couldn't imagine even a hint of suspicion, but even if there was suspicion, there was absolutely no proof. *I'll find out what he thinks he knows*

THIS WASN'T THE HELP I'D PRAYED FOR, BUT I KNEW GOD WAS HELPING ME.

and just keep lying. I have to, for all our sakes.

He continued. "I believe last week when you and your coworker went out of town for that meeting, you did more than just meet with clients. I believe you are having an affair."

My mind raced. *What had happened? How could he know? He couldn't. And who is he to confront me? I'm his boss! I'll just deny it.*

He went on. "I believe you need to see your pastor and confess."

Oh, sure, just walk in and ruin my life and the lives of everyone I care about. Does he not comprehend what he's asking? Does he not realize that he's putting his job in jeopardy?

"If you don't do this, I'll be forced to go." He went on to quote the instructions in Matthew.

Slowly but surely, I realized what courage this young man had mustered to be obedient to God. I realized that God was using him to spur me to action. I was tired of lying. I was tired of running. This wasn't the help I'd prayed for, but I knew God was helping me. I took a deep breath, paused, and exhaled. The fight in me melted away; submission to God came. He wasn't going to let me go on. He wasn't going to let me continue in my sin. He was giving me the nudge I needed to get out of this sin.

"Okay," I said. "I'll call my pastor."

And so began the day that would forever change my life.

MONA'S STORY

(Less than six months after revelation)

I don't think I can stand this anymore, my mind screamed. Here I was again, sitting in church with my two younger sons—alone. And there, just a few rows up and on the right, she sat. Only she wasn't alone. Her husband was with her, and he had his arm around her. Worship? In this church? At this time? How could I worship when my husband's partner sat in the same church? *Oh, Lord, help me.*

My ears could hear the music. My eyes could see people singing. My mind was beginning to panic. Blood rushed to my head. I could feel palpitations in my chest and such anger and vile hatred in my heart. What was I doing here? What kind of a Christian was I?

Then, as if on cue, my boys started to act up—squirming, talking, playing with whatever was at hand. My quiet "reminders" went unheeded. They didn't want to be there, either. This was a mockery.

How many people knew about the affair? I didn't know and would never know. How I wanted to scream at them all, "But he really loves me!" Why would they believe me? I wasn't sure I even believed it. He didn't even sit in church with me. Both he and she had been removed from all public ministries, but my husband was allowed to continue working in the sound booth behind closed doors. It was a

I FELT AS IF I WERE WEARING A SIGN THAT READ "NOT GOOD ENOUGH!"

perfect hiding place for him. And it made me angry. I couldn't hide. I couldn't have him with me. I got the kids—unruly and undisciplined. Anyone who was watching was probably thinking, *Well, we know there are problems in that family.* I felt as if I were wearing a sign that read "NOT GOOD ENOUGH!" Not a good enough wife, not a good enough mother, not a good enough Christian.

The music continued. We stood. We sat. They prayed. I prayed, *Help me!* More music. Announcements. Time to greet. Stand up, shake hands, and smile like nothing was wrong.

"How are you?"

"Fine."

But there they stood. I could still see the happy couple, shaking hands, smiling. Even when I tried to look away, my eyes were irresistibly drawn to them. How could they keep up this façade of normality? How could I?

More music. I couldn't even pretend to sing anymore. I was going crazy. My body surged with adrenalin. I was beginning to cry. *Hide the tears. Don't let the boys see.* "Shhh, be quiet, honey, we're in church."

We sat down. The pastor got up and began to speak. What was he saying? I couldn't hear him. The blood pounded so loudly in my ears I thought everyone around me could hear it, too. *I can't do this. I'm going to be sick.* Vomit rose in my throat. My body shook uncontrollably now.

I'm not hiding this well. I'm losing control. I'm going to stand up and scream like some pitiful, crazy wife from a B movie. I have to get out of here. I can't stay here. But what about my boys? Who will stay with them? What will I tell them? They won't know what to think.

I'll frighten them. Not to mention how they would distract those around us if I left.

This was not the children's fault. We had decided to stay in this church because of them. They had gone here all their lives. Their friends were here. And our oldest was struggling spiritually—we didn't want to help him run from God. If I jumped up and ran out of this church, what would happen to my boys? Weren't they going through enough at home? Besides, we, too, had friends here. We, too, had support here. We'd lost so much already. Did we have to lose our church, too?

♥ ♥

I CAN'T SIT HERE LIKE NOTHING'S WRONG WHEN MY HEART IS BREAKING.

But I can't stay here! I can't sit here like nothing's wrong when my heart is breaking, when my heart is filled with ugly, vile emotions that override my joy and peace. If I sit here any longer, I'm going to be sick. I'm going to lose what is left of my mind. I am dying. I am broken and bleeding just as surely as if someone shot me with a gun. I'm not going to make it.

And then I felt it. An arm around my shoulders. I heard a whisper in my ear, "You're not alone." I knew without looking, there was not another person beside me, yet I could *feel* that arm around me. Maybe I really was crazy. Maybe I had lost it after all. Or maybe what I claimed to believe in was true. I could feel the calm enter my body. Jesus was there with me in that church. I wasn't crazy. He was real, and he was with me. I could feel his arm around me. I could sense his comforting presence telling me I wasn't alone, I would

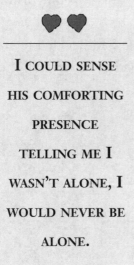

I COULD SENSE HIS COMFORTING PRESENCE TELLING ME I WASN'T ALONE, I WOULD NEVER BE ALONE.

never be alone. He and I would sit there together with these precious children. He and I would go through this entire experience together.

My body calmed down to a level where survival was an option. I may not have heard the sermon, but I did meet my Lord at church that day. And I went home like I did most Sundays, hid in my room, and cried because in a very real sense I had lost my church. It would never be the same again. I would never be the same again. The Lord's presence enabled me to get through that day. He would be faithful to get me through many more days. It did not take all the pain away or solve all the difficulties that came from this sin. He did not make it all right. He did what he promised—he comforted. Just as the healing of my marriage would take time, my faith, too, would grow slowly over time.

THE STORY ON FAITH

When we think of people of great faith, we think of great people. In our thoughts, we paint the picture of a person whose great faith provided a serene smile and a calm demeanor at all times. Hebrews 11 is often called the "hall of faith," yet if you read the Old Testament passages about the people listed in that chapter, you will find they were just ordinary people who struggled with personal weaknesses and failures in the midst of life's circumstances. What set them apart was that they learned what "living by faith" meant. And that was also what made a difference in our recovery.

FAITH IS ...

Let's define the word *faith* before we go on. It's one of those words that often means different things to different people. The simplest, most accurate definition is that faith is believing what God says to the extent that it influences your thinking *and* your behavior. Faith gives your belief substance and makes belief a tangible thing. It is by faith that we act. Hebrews 11 is full of "by faith" this or that was done.

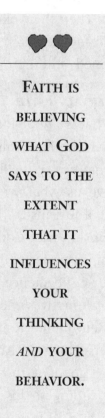

FAITH IS BELIEVING WHAT GOD SAYS TO THE EXTENT THAT IT INFLUENCES YOUR THINKING *AND* YOUR BEHAVIOR.

Let's look at God's definition of faith in Hebrews 11:1. "Now faith is being sure of what we hope for and certain of what we do not see."

The problems often come when we misplace our hope. During our recovery, we often "hoped" we would wake up and find the adultery had never happened. In fact, Mona had just such a dream. She dreamed she woke up in the intensive care unit, and standing there were Gary and his partner. They looked very concerned. She looked up at them, shocked they were both there, and said, "You can't see each other. You can't be here together!" They looked surprised and asked why. Incredulously, Mona said, "Because of your affair."

They looked at her, smiled, and said, "Mona, that never happened. You were dreaming. You've been sick and in the hospital." It took some convincing, but other people came into the room and backed up everything they were saying until finally, blessedly, she believed them. And then a profound sense of relief and peace flooded her body. It never had happened.

Then she woke up. She was in her own bedroom, and the old familiar pain still gripped her heart. It really had happened, and there was no relief or peace in that.

CERTAIN FAITH

What we hope for in faith and are certain of is what God has said. We have faith that he is who he says he is and can do what he says he'll do. God is not a vending machine that will give us what we want—even what we think we need—if we'll just insert the right "faith" coin. The core of our relationship with God is love between him and us. That relationship is perfected in our obedience and severely disrupted by our disobedience.

Jesus was the perfect example of that relationship. The often-quoted Romans 8:28 is incomplete without verse 29. Verse 28 says, "And we know that in all things God works for the good of those who love him, who have been called according to his purpose." Then verse 29 continues, "For those God foreknew he also predestined to be conformed to the likeness of his Son, that he might be the firstborn among many brothers."

GROWING FAITH

God's purpose is that we would be like Jesus. Nowhere does it say his purpose is to make us healthy, wealthy, and happy.

Jesus came as a servant sent here for the salvation of humankind. The point was to provide the bridge so God could have a relationship with us. It's about God. It's not about us. God will use whatever serves his purpose to enhance his relationship with us, to make us more like Jesus, who had the perfect relationship with the Father. Within that relationship, we receive joy and peace, irrespective of our circumstances.

Bearing these truths in mind, we would like to share with you the beliefs that made the difference in our recovery.

OUR FAITH GREW BECAUSE WE FOUND THAT GOD IS ENOUGH

We, along with many others with whom we have discussed this issue, have found God sufficient only when he was all we had. Not that he wasn't sufficient before, only that we hadn't ever realized it.

Mona grasped this truth one evening after yet another extended time of talking, tears, and pain. As she stood in the doorway between the bedroom and master bath, she suddenly collapsed onto the floor. "This is killing me, and I really don't think I'm going to make it through." She suddenly realized she

> GOD GAVE MONA THE KNOWLEDGE THAT SHE WOULD SURVIVE—NOT THAT EVERYTHING WOULD BE OKAY, BUT THAT HE WOULD ENABLE HER TO SURVIVE.

had lost not only her marriage and her husband, but also part of herself.

There was absolutely nothing left to hang on to. She found herself completely insufficient for the first time in her life, and terror gripped her. That night, God gave Mona the knowledge that she would survive—not that everything would be okay, but that he would enable her to survive. She would be okay whether or not the marriage healed. She wanted the marriage to survive, but if it didn't, she would survive.

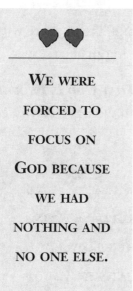

WE WERE FORCED TO FOCUS ON GOD BECAUSE WE HAD NOTHING AND NO ONE ELSE.

Also during this time, she came to understand that she had put Gary above God. It was not that she thought Gary was God—especially now—but she looked to Gary to be her source of strength, comfort, and love. What she learned was that Gary would fail in that regard. Mona had failed when Gary had expected her to be the same for him. It was a role God never intended for any human being to perform. We are all incapable of fulfilling it. Life would be easier, better even, with Gary as her husband, but he wasn't necessary for her survival.

We were forced to focus on God because we had nothing and no one else. Even those who loved us and knew what was happening were incapable of fully meeting our needs. This understanding came at great cost, but it is a lesson that we wouldn't trade. It focused both of us on our relationship with the Lord and who is first and most important in our lives. In understanding this, we received the benefit of an environment conducive to healing and eventually a healthier marriage. We understood Paul's words in 2 Corinthians 12:9: "But he said to me, 'My grace is sufficient for you, for my power is made perfect in weakness.'"

Our faith grew because we found we were not enough and God was.

OUR FAITH GREW BECAUSE GOD NEVER LEFT US

That day in church Mona learned that God had never left her. In the worst of times, an aloneness penetrated our souls, but it also provided us with an opportunity to realize God's continuing presence. Can we leave God? You bet. Whenever we turn our backs and disobey, we walk away from him. But he is always there, waiting for our return. Our relationship with the Lord is the only truly secure relationship we'll ever have.

Gary experienced this reality in the midst of his adultery. God chases us and woos us back. He is always there ready, willing, and able to reestablish that relationship he so desires with us. Gary had made the mistake, committed the sin, effectively turning his back. But God chased him throughout it all. Gary had cried out repeatedly to God, "Help me! Help me!" And God would. He would tell Gary the way out was to confess and repent, just as he'd told people from the beginning of time. He used books, sermons, conversations, and any number of things. The answer continued to get clearer in Gary's mind. The conviction of knowing the relationship was a sinful one would not leave. The truth that there was no future for either party in a sinful relationship would not leave. Gary got caught in what he calls the "confession deception." He would fall. He would cry out to God and confess with the intention of never falling again. Then as time went by, he would fall again, and the cycle would repeat. God kept chasing him. The truth of Matthew 5:29–30 became clear. "If your right eye causes you to sin, gouge it out and throw it away. It is better for you to lose one part of your body than for your whole body to be thrown into hell. And if your right hand causes you to sin, cut it off and throw it away. It is better for you to lose one part of your body than for your whole body to go into hell."

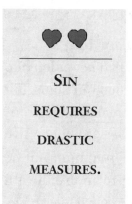

SIN REQUIRES DRASTIC MEASURES.

The point here is not self-mutilation, but rather that sin requires drastic measures. Gary had to do something drastic, or sin would continue to have its hold on his life. The "confession deception" cycle was revealed repeatedly for its impotence. God kept telling Gary, *Whatever it takes, do it. Come back to me; I'm here with open arms.* Only later did we realize the context of Matthew 5:29–30. Jesus was talking about adultery in the preceding two verses.

Becoming aware that God would indeed never leave us or forsake us (Hebrews 13:5) allowed us to experience the reality of his sufficiency.

Our faith grew because God never left us.

OUR FAITH GREW BECAUSE WE LEARNED THE TRUTH ABOUT GOD'S COMFORT

Somewhere we had gotten the idea that if God comforts us, then the pain goes away and the circumstances right themselves. Mona once heard a retreat speaker clarify that false thinking like this: "God promises to comfort us. The problem is we want to be comfortable." The truth of that statement hit solidly home at this point in our lives. Mona was angry with God, impatiently waiting for him to do his "comforting."

GOD COMFORTS US *IN* OUR TROUBLES, NOT *OUT* OF THEM.

When she finally understood the truth—that God comforts us *in* our troubles, not *out* of them—she saw how often he'd been there, comforting her. Like that day at church, like later that day when she finally could pull herself up off the bed, and every single instance when he had used someone or something to help get her through one more hour.

We all want the pain to go away. We want it to be over and let us have our lives back. Sin truly is ugly and pervasive. Fortunately, because of Jesus, God forgives our sin, and we can have a love relationship with him. Unfortunately, the consequences of our sin remain. Some consequences will be temporary and perhaps not too severe. Other consequences will have a life of their own, and we will be freed from them only at heaven's gates. Through it all, however, we have the promise of God's comfort. "Praise be to the God and Father of our Lord Jesus Christ, the Father of compassion and the God of all comfort, who comforts us in all our troubles" (2 Corinthians 1:3–4).

OUR FAITH GREW BECAUSE A FAITHFUL GOD COMFORTS US

Our faith became a reality and enabled us to heal. If we had not leaned on God, we would have been tossed about like a rowboat in a hurricane. We have observed other couples in our groups being tossed about as well. If we can help keep your time in the hurricane to a minimum, then our goal has been accomplished. Don't get us wrong. None of this is easy. It took everything we had just to keep putting one foot in front of the other each day. There was no magic formula, just absolute and profound truth. Choosing to believe the truth is the foundation of faith. That truth is available to all of us in the Word of God. He is faithful. He is trustworthy. He is the rock our faith can rest on.

> **THERE WAS NO MAGIC FORMULA, JUST ABSOLUTE AND PROFOUND TRUTH.**

THREE

ADMITTING OUR ROLES

The LORD is near to all who call on him,
to all who call on him in truth.

PSALM 145:18

MONA'S STORY

(Less than one year after revelation)

The intervals between counseling sessions seemed like years to me. Our counselor was busy, and sometimes we had difficulty scheduling as frequently as we wanted. Strangely, I hadn't even wanted to go for counseling in the beginning, but now I couldn't wait to get there. It was the only place we could really talk about what had happened with another person. Our families didn't know, so we had to pretend everything was fine when we were with them. At church, other than the pastor, the deacon board, and a couple of close friends, we didn't know who else knew what was going on in our lives.

I so often wished there were little flashing neon signs on

the foreheads of those who knew. I'm not sure what good it would have done, but I wanted desperately to know who knew about this most intimate part of my life. Who saw me and thought what? Did they think, *Poor Mona. She didn't do anything to deserve this,* or did they think, *Poor Gary. We saw it coming; she must be so difficult to live with*?

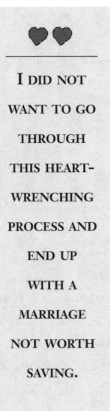

I DID NOT WANT TO GO THROUGH THIS HEART-WRENCHING PROCESS AND END UP WITH A MARRIAGE NOT WORTH SAVING.

And God only knew what they thought of Gary. He said he could tell who knew—especially the women. They treated him differently now, and they didn't want their husbands with him. The fact that Gary's partner walked these same church halls only enriched their imaginations. No, there was no one we could really talk to—only each other and our counselor.

We needed outside input. Who knew if either one of us even had the capacity to see things clearly anymore. And we needed someone who had some idea of what we were dealing with.

I wanted to do this right. I wanted this to count for something. I did not want to go through this heart-wrenching process and end up with a marriage not worth saving. The possibility of going through this pain and torment to be just another statistic was more than I could handle. And just how were we to deal with the previous twenty years of marriage? Were they worthless? Was our marriage a sham from day one? I couldn't believe that. We loved each other! We had been happy!

I dragged my thoughts back to the present and focused on today's counseling session. As painful as these times were, at least we discussed the adultery. Even all these months later I still had difficulty believing we were going through this. Never in my wildest dreams had I thought we'd ever deal with adultery. I sat there while we got through the pleasantries, thinking, *Come on, let's get on with this; we only have fifty minutes.*

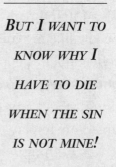

BUT I WANT TO KNOW WHY I HAVE TO DIE WHEN THE SIN IS NOT MINE!

The counselor asked how we were doing. *How are we doing? What does he think? My heart has been ripped from my chest. There's a bleeding, gaping wound that may or may not heal. Gary looks in the mirror and sees a despicable person, a liar, and a cheat. Or at least I think that's what he sees. I look at Gary, and I don't know what I see anymore. God, I need a miracle here. You are the great Healer. Heal us! Let me wake up from this nightmare. We're sitting here breathing, and yet as surely as there is air moving in and out of my lungs, I know we're dying. But I want to know why I have to die when the sin is not mine! I didn't do this. Gary did this. She did this. I know I wasn't a perfect wife, but who is? Gary hasn't been a perfect husband, either. Isn't that what marriage is about—loving and respecting in spite of imperfections?*

The conversations—both in my head and in the counselor's office—were not going as I wanted. We were discussing everything but the adultery. I remembered that in an earlier session the counselor had suggested a book on codependency. I had almost laughed out loud. My faults lay in control, not the pitiful "How can I please my man?" mentality. I had looked at him and asked, "You think I'm codependent?" Calmly he looked directly at me and said, "I know you are."

Well, I'd taken that book home to prove him wrong. But I read it and realized he was probably right. I hadn't realized people like me could be called codependent. I always thought codependent people were the ones being controlled, not the ones doing the controlling. I'd also seen some interesting things about my relationship with my father, how he had urged me to play a role in his life I should never have played. It was nothing sexual, but inappropriate just the same. That

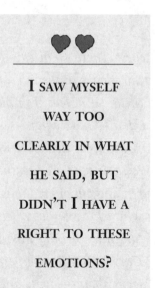

I SAW MYSELF WAY TOO CLEARLY IN WHAT HE SAID, BUT DIDN'T I HAVE A RIGHT TO THESE EMOTIONS?

was all interesting enough, but that was not why we were here, and I didn't want to digress again. If he handed me another book, I was going to scream!

The counselor grabbed another book. Only this time it was a Bible. How could I object to that one? I claimed to be a Christian. I claimed to love this book. But I already knew what God said about adultery. Didn't this guy realize how desperate we were for help?

He opened it and read Ephesians 4:31–32. "Get rid of all bitterness, rage and anger, brawling and slander, along with every form of malice. Be kind and compassionate to one another, forgiving each other, just as in Christ God forgave you."

This wasn't about adultery. It wasn't even about marriage. We were going to get a lesson on forgiveness. Didn't this guy understand the wound of adultery?

He pulled out a tablet and wrote down the words: *bitterness, rage, anger, brawling, slander,* and *malice.* He proceeded to define them. My visual of a barroom brawl was replaced by a visual of an angry person, boiling over, yelling, crying, using words that caused injury. Did I really need this? I saw myself way too clearly in what he said, but didn't I have a right to these emotions? Look at what had been done to me!

The counselor went on to talk about repetitive patterns and how people respond to them. He talked about the hurt these behaviors caused. *Wait a minute; we're not talking about just since revelation of the adultery, are we! We're talking about how two people interact. Let's be honest; we're talking about me. We're dissecting Mona as a person, Mona as a wife. Why am I the one being examined and revealed? I haven't committed adultery! Am I not suffering enough? Are you going to beat me down until I'm just a spot on the floor? Until I no longer exist at all?*

He drew two stick figures and wrote the words *critical spirit* between them. He agreed that only the Lord could meet all the needs of another person, yet he instructed us in his Word on how to treat one another. The counselor went on to define *kindness, compassion,* and a *forgiving spirit.*

The conviction of that drawing, those definitions, was overwhelming. I could barely speak. I wasn't a shrew. But I did have a critical spirit. It slipped out sometimes. And maybe I didn't even try to hold it in at home. More important, I knew Gary had experienced my critical spirit much too often. He didn't think he was even important to me anymore. How could he think that? *God, please tell me this didn't happen because of how I've treated him.* I was just tired. I had three active little boys, one of whom was a challenging child in every situation. I had a demanding, stressful job. Somewhere along the line, I had run out of resources, run out of desire, run out of kindness and compassion for my husband. I had figured Gary loved me enough, knew me well enough, to understand that our time would come later. What was that saying? "Life is what happens while you're making other plans."

Had Gary's life gone on while I'd planned for a future? Had he taken his "unmet needs" elsewhere? Mona had been a bad wife, so poor Gary had to go to someone else? I felt rage growing inside me. I felt myself puffing up with indignation. And then suddenly I knew the truth. *Oh God, I wasn't really that bad, was I? I didn't really cause this, did I?*

I don't remember if I actually verbalized the question, but I do remember the answer. "There will never be a good enough reason for what Gary chose to do. There will never be a good enough reason for the adultery." The counselor went on to explain that Gary's choosing adultery was his way of dealing with our problems. However, if

> I KNEW IF WE WERE GOING TO HEAL COMPLETELY, WE WOULD HAVE TO LOOK AT OURSELVES, AT WHAT "WE" HAD BECOME.

we really wanted to heal, we would need to identify those problems and deal with them together, in a healthy way.

I resisted. I didn't want to look at and identify our issues as a couple. There was already so much pain in just dealing with the adultery. But I knew if we were going to heal completely, we would have to look at ourselves, at what "we" had become. We had to give each other hope that this journey would be worth it.

God, give me the strength.

GARY'S STORY

(Less than six months after revelation)

"Where is the anger?"

I looked at my Christian counselor, his head cocked to one side, his forehead crinkled, and a very determined, pondering look on his face as he repeated himself. "Where is the anger?"

This was one of my first sessions alone with him. I had just spilled my guts, saying, "How could I have done this to such a perfect wife? How could I have been so selfish?"

But he just kept staring at me and asked again, "Where is the anger?"

What is he talking about? I'm the bad guy here. What in the world did I have to be angry about? I didn't have any right to be angry! I was the black-hearted liar. The cheat. The adulterer!

I asked him what he meant. He smiled and explained, "I just don't see the anger here. I know it's there. Nobody does what you did without it. You must be angry about something Mona did or didn't do. You aren't being honest with yourself if you deny that she had anything to do with all this."

"Wait a minute!" I said. "This isn't her fault. I'm the one who had the affair."

"Yes, you did," he agreed. "But a relationship is a two-sided thing. If you really want to heal your marriage, you're going to have to stop blaming yourself and start looking at your relationship honestly from top to bottom."

YOU'RE GOING TO HAVE TO STOP BLAMING YOURSELF AND START LOOKING AT YOUR RELATIONSHIP HONESTLY FROM TOP TO BOTTOM.

It was about time to wrap up the session. He told me to go home and do some soul-searching. He wanted me to get alone with God and ask him to reveal to my heart the absolute truth about Mona's and my relationship.

And so I did. I prayed that God would reveal truth to me. As I prayed, I kept thinking of a time when Mona and I were in the kitchen. I don't remember what we were talking about at the time, but we had the dogs and the kids underfoot as usual. The decibel level was a little too high for my taste, but that's the way it is with three rowdy boys, so I had just learned to live with it.

I remember coming up behind Mona while she was stirring the spaghetti sauce on the stove. As I placed my hands on her hips, I felt her stiffen and pull away. I looked at her, and she was frowning at me. I leaned over to give her a kiss.

She leaned slightly toward me, never closing her eyes, and gave me a stiff-necked "grandma" peck on the lips.

"Our time will come later," she said.

Her reaction had pricked my heart. "Okay," I said with a smirk and went back to my seat at the kitchen table. I really hadn't thought much about it until a week later when we were entertaining friends for dinner. All the kids were off in the family room playing. The four adults were sitting around the kitchen table, talking and shar-

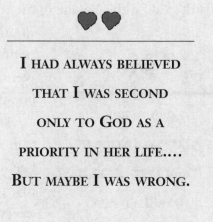

I HAD ALWAYS BELIEVED THAT I WAS SECOND ONLY TO GOD AS A PRIORITY IN HER LIFE.... BUT MAYBE I WAS WRONG.

ing stories about the rigors of raising children. She said it again. "Our time will come later." This time I really heard her, and the words cut me like a knife.

I understood what she meant. She was saying that once the kids were grown, once all the important jobs were done, once everything in life that had real meaning was taken care of, then and only then would there be time for us, for me. I was low man on the totem pole in her life. I asked myself how I had gotten so low on her priority list, and then I just filed the incidents away.

At the time, I had rationalized she couldn't possibly mean it the way I'd heard it. But the more I prayed now, the more those pictures, those words, returned to my mind. "Our time will come later." I had always believed that I was second only to God as a priority in her life. Then came the kids, and after them came everything else. But maybe I was wrong.

I had filed those interactions with her in a dark and hidden place in my heart, where they had festered. I had been angry! I was angry now! How could I have not seen this truth? Could this be one of the reasons I had been vulnerable to adultery? Did I feel so unimportant in my wife's life that I went out and tried to fill that emptiness with someone else?

The more I thought about it, the more I realized what had been lying under the surface in my mind. Mona had had time for everyone else—her kids, her family, her friends, her church, her work, her Bible study, her social life. Everyone and everything but me!

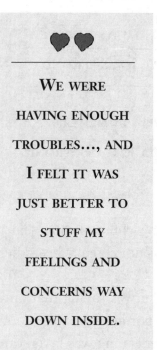

WE WERE HAVING ENOUGH TROUBLES..., AND I FELT IT WAS JUST BETTER TO STUFF MY FEELINGS AND CONCERNS WAY DOWN INSIDE.

Wait just a minute. If I had really been bothered that much, why didn't I just go to Mona, sit her down, and have a heart-to-heart? I knew the answer to that question. I am the epitome of a conflict-avoider. And at this low point in our relationship, I would have done anything to avoid conflict. We were having enough troubles with our kids, and I felt it was just better to stuff my feelings and concerns way down inside and try to forget about them rather than make things even more uncomfortable and try to work them out.

I hadn't known how vulnerable I was. I never intended to have an affair. I never thought I ever would. And then along came a person who listened to me and cared about my problems. She was having problems in her marriage also, so we could help each other. We never had any intention beyond being two caring Christians helping one another along the terrible path of being a neglected spouse. One step followed another and another, and before I knew it, it had happened. I was caught up in an affair.

OUR COUNSELOR HAD BEEN RIGHT. I *WAS* ANGRY.

Even as I thought these things through, I knew I had no excuse for my behavior. There is no reason good enough to justify adultery. But perhaps this was one of the reasons I could identify as I began this long, soul-searching, difficult process of what I was to eventually call "peeling the onion"—removing the outer layers of our relationship, trying to comprehend what had happened to us. Trying to heal.

God had started revealing to me the absolute truth I was praying for. Our counselor had been right. I *was* angry.

THE STORY ON ADMITTING OUR ROLES

Whenever we get to this point in our groups, we can see the various reactions on all the faces. We can almost hear the thoughts bouncing off the walls. *Don't even try to tell me this is my fault!* the spouse is thinking. And the infidel asks, "I just destroyed our relationship, and now I'm supposed to sit here and tell my spouse what I don't like about him or her?"

THERE IS NO REASON GOOD ENOUGH TO JUSTIFY ADULTERY. ADMITTING OUR ROLES IN THE DECLINE OF OUR MARRIAGES IS NOT "THE ANSWER" FOR WHY THE ADULTERY HAPPENED.

Both in their own way are saying, "Let's stick to reality and talk about the adultery!"

Let us again reassure you: there is no reason good enough to justify adultery. Admitting our roles in the decline of our marriages is not "the answer" for why the adultery happened. It is a compilation of behaviors, attitudes, and responses that you have allowed within your relationship that were not and still are not conducive to a healthy marriage.

Just as surely as God instructs us in his Word how to treat other people, he also tells us how to handle problems with people. Perhaps if we were wiser, we'd focus on the former and have no need for the latter. But we're people, and people make mistakes. People hurt the people closest to them. And if you are reading this, then there have been some significant hurts in your marriage. Sometimes the greatest hurts are accomplished by not saying anything or by our reactions when something is said.

WASHING WOUNDS

When our children were little and one of them suffered a scrape, Mona the nurse would always take him in and wash the cut. This was never a fun time. Washing a scrape hurts. Our son wanted to just leave it alone or at most run water on it. He never wanted his mother to actually touch the thing. Mona would then explain if he wanted it to hurt a lot more, he could leave it alone and let it get infected. The choice was little pain now or big pain later; he could choose.

We have the same option over and over in our marriages: little pain now or big pain later. Many of us choose big pain later, and we often get more hurt than we ever bargained for.

This sounds like spilled milk or sour grapes, you may be thinking. How does looking backward help healing after adultery? Let us offer what we've learned about "cleaning the scrapes" that will help you in your journey toward rebuilding your marriage.

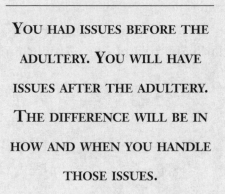

YOU HAD ISSUES BEFORE THE ADULTERY. YOU WILL HAVE ISSUES AFTER THE ADULTERY. THE DIFFERENCE WILL BE IN HOW AND WHEN YOU HANDLE THOSE ISSUES.

ROLE RESOLUTION

You had issues within your marriage before the adultery. You will have issues after the adultery. The difference will be in how and when you handle those issues. Some of the bigger problems we had, such as where Gary`was on Mona's priority list, needed immediate attention. But some just needed to be discussed and allowed to exist within our relationship.

For example, Mona wanted Gary to plan surprises. She felt Gary could show her how much he cared by taking the time to do something for her simply because he knew how much it would please her. She wanted him to take care of all the details and do it well. For her birthday, ten months after revelation, we were going to go to the ocean for the weekend. Mona wanted Gary to plan it, and he offered to do so. This would be a new way he could show her love. The end result was both of us sitting on our bed the night before we left in tears with no hotel reservations. Everything nice was booked. Gary felt like a jerk who had failed yet again. Mona was disappointed because her preconceived weekend didn't materialize.

In the end, we went, we stayed in a so-so place, and we clarified a part of our relationship. Gary is not a planner. He never has been. Mona is. She is detail oriented and thinks things through. Neither Gary's lack of planning nor Mona's ability to plan has anything to do with our love for each other. Therefore, Mona became the official planner for the family. She would not take offense at Gary's lack of planning, and he would not consider her planning a control issue. They would discuss ideas, she'd research, come back for discussion and agreement, and then she would book. It has worked

NOT ALL ISSUES WILL BE RESOLVED THE WAY YOU MAY HAVE ENVISIONED. NEVERTHELESS, YOU NEED TO DISCUSS THEM.

well since. Now neither of us is disappointed, and we spend our time away enjoying each other.

The point is that not all issues will be resolved the way you may have envisioned. Nevertheless, you need to discuss them. It took some honest conversation and some changes in our thinking for us to understand the other's expectations on the planning issue. You will need to do the same within your marriage. And don't worry about whether anyone else has solved the problem the way you do. If your solution works for your relationship and you are in agreement, stop there.

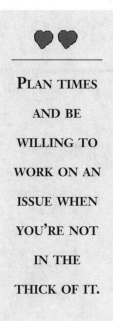

PLAN TIMES AND BE WILLING TO WORK ON AN ISSUE WHEN YOU'RE NOT IN THE THICK OF IT.

Sometimes when the kids had those scrapes we mentioned earlier, the washing occurred when they took their baths at bedtime. Fighting the cleaning battle when they were going back outside to play for a couple more hours seemed senseless. Trying to discuss certain relationship issues when you are emotionally exhausted, angry, or hurt can be senseless, too. Plan times and be willing to work on an issue when you're not in the thick of it. And yes, it may not be the most fun you'll have as a couple. But we believe it will facilitate many more fun times in the long run. Think of it as defusing a bomb Satan would love to plant in your home. Obviously, not every issue will be a onetime discussion. It's a marriage-for-a-lifetime plan. And only the two of you can really decide which issues can be allowed to exist within your relationship and which need to be dealt with and eliminated.

A MATTER OF OPINION

Open your ears! Sometimes we don't hear ourselves very well. Mona didn't really comprehend what she was conveying to Gary when she said, "Our time will come later." But what she meant wasn't important. What Gary heard and understood was that he didn't really matter, and that became reality. Mona felt overwhelmed by her responsibilities at that time and thought that Gary would understand that she wanted to pay attention to him when she could really focus on him without the distraction of family and work. She wasn't making a conscious choice to lower Gary on the list. It happened insidiously. Mona didn't wake up one day and say, "I don't care about Gary," just as Gary didn't wake up one day and say, "I think I'll have an affair and destroy my life."

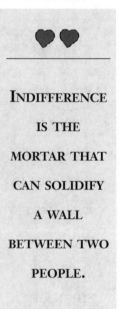

INDIFFERENCE IS THE MORTAR THAT CAN SOLIDIFY A WALL BETWEEN TWO PEOPLE.

It's been said that if Satan can't get you to sin, he'll keep you busy. We suggest that this is most often the case at home in our marriages. Indifference is the mortar that can solidify a wall between two people, who one day come to their senses and face an impenetrable barrier.

You can avoid building walls by caring enough to raise issues you find troubling, to honestly express how you see things. Care enough to listen without getting defensive. Care enough to find a way back to each other. You already know what can happen when you try to avoid pain. Be thankful for little pain now. But give your spouse the consideration that communicates, "I value you enough to listen to your perspective even if I don't see it the same way." And then do it. Listen!

We all want to express ourselves. We all want to explain why the situation really isn't as bad as the other person sees it, why we really didn't mean what our spouse thinks we meant. We want to fix the misconception or even deny the wrong. That approach is not likely to solve the problem. If your spouse perceives an event or conversation differently than you do, the perception he or she has is real and requires your respect. However, it doesn't make either of you right or wrong.

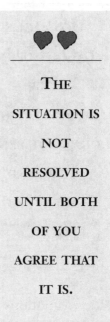

THE SITUATION IS NOT RESOLVED UNTIL BOTH OF YOU AGREE THAT IT IS.

When you both understand the problem—when you have both heard the other—together you can find a solution that works for both of you. Sometimes Gary just gave up something that wasn't really important because Mona's viewpoint felt important to her, and sometimes it would be the other way around. Sometimes Mona agreed not to take things so personally and to remember our discussions, and sometimes it would be the other way around. We both learned to flex where we could.

The point is that this is your marriage; the two of you have to live with your decisions, so the situation is not resolved until both of you agree that it is.

DON'T AVOID THE ISSUES

Unfortunately, we have had couples in our groups who avoid the issues festering in their relationship. Years before, there had been a first incident of adultery, or even an instance of an improper attraction, and they had to admit they really hadn't dealt with either the incident itself or the events that led up

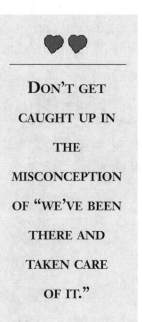

DON'T GET CAUGHT UP IN THE MISCONCEPTION OF "WE'VE BEEN THERE AND TAKEN CARE OF IT."

to it. So five, ten, even twenty years later, it happened again. Sad to say, we've even had couples go through our groups and still resist addressing their issues. "We really don't have any," they both say with conviction. Yet, after intensive time spent in our group setting, it's easy for us to see some of the issues from the other side of the table. Our hearts grieve, and we pray that God will reveal to them whatever work needs to be done.

Sometimes bad timing gets in the way of couples confronting their issues. Immediately after revelation, emotions are in turmoil and on overload. Hearts are raw and wounded. Looking at roles in the marriage, at issues in the relationship, can come later when you've gotten a little foothold again.

Let us caution you, however. While it can be easy to get comfortable and welcome any semblance of normalcy, don't get caught up in the misconception of "we've been there and taken care of it." The issues you'll deal with took a long time to come to the surface, and they won't be resolved with one or two conversations. We encourage you not to lose sight of the necessity of confronting your pain. Be afraid. Be very afraid of what can happen if you do not deal with these things. Resist the temptation to avoid the pain. Even when you make changes after going through adultery recovery, unresolved issues will follow you wherever you go.

Trust God to handle your pain as you face the problems that led you to the crisis you're now in. He got you through the revelation; he can get you through the rest.

Finally, don't be afraid to come back to something after you thought it had been dealt with. Revisiting an issue doesn't mean your marriage is on the rocks again; it simply means you are now aware and you care about keeping your relationship smooth. You may need clarification on a particular point, or you may just want to check in with each other to see if your solution is still satisfactory to you both.

> **DON'T BE AFRAID TO COME BACK TO SOMETHING AFTER YOU THOUGHT IT HAD BEEN DEALT WITH.**

Your marriage relationship is the most important human relationship you will have. It deserves every ounce of energy and love you put into it.

FOUR

NEVER GOING BACK

I will listen to what God the Lord will say;
he promises peace to his people, his saints—
but let them not return to folly.
PSALM 85:8

GARY'S STORY

(Less than one year after revelation)

The spa on our deck had become a different place these last few months. What used to be family time with the kids had turned into couple time with Mona and me trying to work through the chaos of our lives.

It had rained earlier that evening, and steam rose slowly from the water. I felt like a prune because we had been there for well over an hour, "talking it through" again. I could see that every question she asked and every answer I offered sent her trudging deeper into the pit of depression. I was growing more and more concerned that she was ever going to pull out of it. I knew God was with us, but I didn't know how we were ever going to get past this horrible darkness.

I prayed, *God, what do I do? How do I answer her? Should I be honest? Even if I hurt her?*

God answered me with another question. *Do you want to go back to the way it was?*

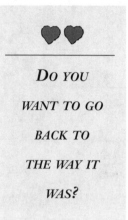

Do you

want to go

back to

the way it

was?

No! That was one question I didn't have trouble with. The way our marriage was hadn't been good enough to save us from this. The way it was didn't keep me from drifting away. I absolutely did not want our relationship to go back to the way it had been! If we were going to go through the pain and agony of peeling this onion, of getting down to the real problems of our relationship, honestly and tearfully asking and answering the hard questions that would bring about real healing, then I couldn't take the easy way out now. Taking the easy way had brought us to this place, and I knew I didn't want to stay here any longer.

Mona gently interrupted my prayers and thoughts, asking the one question I had dreaded more than any other, the question that required an answer I knew she would probably not understand. "Will you ever do this again?"

"No, of course not!" should have been my instant answer. But I couldn't say it, so I hesitated. I knew I had to be honest, and I really didn't know whether I would or wouldn't do it again. I couldn't tell the future. I didn't know. I had pledged my faithfulness at our wedding with great sincerity and had not kept that promise. I didn't want to ever again make a promise I could not keep. I tried to explain my hesitation, but it was too late.

She was instantly outraged. She screamed at me, "You can't tell me you'll never do it again?"

I kept trying to explain. "I don't know the future. And if I am going to be absolutely honest with you, I can't just say what we both want to hear."

That wasn't good enough. She stormed into the house, crying. When I finally caught up with her in the bedroom, she was in bed, the lights were off, and the room was completely silent. I tried to talk, but it wasn't going to happen. She was shut down, turned inward, and totally engulfed in her own abyss.

I feared what she was thinking. How could I be honest and not cause more pain? After trying again and again to draw her out of her silence, I finally gave up. Maybe time and rest would help.

The morning brings a new day, but not that morning. I woke up next to a woman emotionally detached from me and everyone else. She didn't say a word except what was absolutely necessary to get the kids ready for school. Once they were set, I took them to school and returned home.

I barely got through the door before she said, "We need to go to the counselor now!" I had never seen her like this. She was hard as steel, cold and determined. "You make the appointment, or I will," she said. "In fact, you don't even have to go, but I do."

I tried to talk about last night's unresolved conversation, but she stopped me before I even got out five words.

"Okay, fine. I'll make the appointment myself!" she said.

I assured her I did want to go with her, and so I called. I told the counselor's delightfully cheery receptionist we needed an appointment today, and I wasn't kidding. "It's today or perhaps never again." On hold I went, and within seconds she was back. "Ten o'clock okay?"

"Perfect," I replied, and I thanked God for providing.

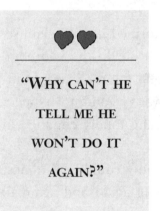

"WHY CAN'T HE TELL ME HE WON'T DO IT AGAIN?"

Ten o'clock was only a couple of hours away, but it seemed like an eternity. I resisted the urge to turn on the radio to drown out the silence on the trip to the office. I think we were in the waiting room only about thirty seconds before the door opened and our counselor stepped out, smiling. He took one look at Mona and stopped smiling.

Once behind the closed door of his office, Mona didn't wait for any formalities. "He can't say he won't do it again! I can't do this anymore. I don't think we're going to make it. I think we have to separate." Then she broke. "Why can't he tell me he won't do it again?" Tears streamed down her face. "Why?"

The counselor directed his attention to me. "Gary, are you planning to commit adultery again?"

I replied without any hesitation, "No, of course not!"

"Then why can't you tell her you won't do it again?"

I began to explain. "I am not going back to the way it was. I am not going to tell Mona what I think she wants to hear or not tell her something I want to say, just to avoid dealing with her reaction. I am only going to tell Mona the absolute truth.

I can't predict the future, so therefore I can't say with absolute honesty I will never do it again. I thought I'd never do it in the first place."

I watched our counselor relax just a bit. Then without missing a beat, he repeated his question, "Are you planning on doing this again?"

"No, of course not!" I said again, more emphatically.

He then turned to Mona. "Can you hear what Gary is saying?" I watched as her troubled and overwhelmed mind tried to assimilate what was happening. I saw a sense of understanding begin to dawn across her face.

Oh, Mona, please understand. I'm not saying I can't tell you I'll never do it again because I want to give myself permission. I only want to be completely honest with you and with myself. I don't want to break another promise to you ever again. I want to someday be able to talk with you honestly and not see pain envelop you. I want us to survive. I can't go back to who I was; therefore, we can never go back to who we were.

Mona's Story

(Less than one year after revelation)

"I will not do this again! Do you hear me? I will never, ever do this again!" The high-pitched, passionate, and loud voice I heard was my own. I was furious, and screaming at my husband seemed to be the only way to let him know how I felt. Gary looked so very weary, and our three young sons were in a nearby room, undoubtedly terrified and unsure of how to respond to my tirade.

What had happened to our family? What was happening? This was so wrong. I stormed down the hall to my room and closed the door, effectively, once again, ruining any chance of a "normal" evening.

Since the night Gary had told me about his adultery, time had rearranged itself. It was all divided into "before the affair," "during the affair," and "after the affair." I didn't know which time was worse. *Before* was a sham, a fraud I had perpetuated. Had he ever loved me? What else had been a lie? *During* was nothing but being lied to and being so very stupid. How many times and in how many ways had I implied or even outright commented on what a good marriage we had to my "friend," his partner? *After* was hell. Plain and simple. Pain, every day, all day. I was incapable of being a good mother, a good friend, a good employee. Anytime there was a moment's release from it, I made sure it didn't last long.

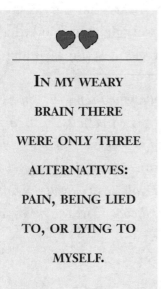

IN MY WEARY BRAIN THERE WERE ONLY THREE ALTERNATIVES: PAIN, BEING LIED TO, OR LYING TO MYSELF.

In my weary brain there were only three alternatives: pain, being lied to, or lying to myself. If there was no pain, then someone was lying. At least the pain was real, or so I thought. In one of her books, author Barbara Johnson wrote about a home for the bewildered. That was where I needed to go. My tears had far outnumbered my smiles for a very long time.

How long had it been like this? I could tell you exactly how long it had been since that night Gary had walked into our bedroom and confessed his affair of three years with my best Christian friend. What I didn't know was how much longer the pain would go on. How much more could our family take?

Gary was ready for peace; he needed some peace. Well, too bad. My peace was gone, too. But what about my boys? Didn't they deserve some time without turmoil? Was I to live a lie so my children could have peace? It was all so intense. I couldn't figure anything out anymore. I couldn't even take care of my children. I was going nuts. If Gary's adultery didn't destroy us, it looked like my craziness would.

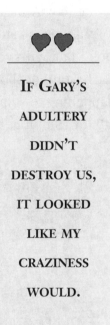

IF GARY'S ADULTERY DIDN'T DESTROY US, IT LOOKED LIKE MY CRAZINESS WOULD.

That night, Gary had been late coming home. I had looked at the clock every couple of minutes and thought about what could be delaying him. He hadn't answered the phone at the office. Then I thought about where he could be, who he could be with. I trembled, and the blood drained from my face. I started to panic. Then a rational thought came: *If I start responding like this every time he is late, I will spend the rest of my life doing it.* Every minute Gary was unaccounted for, I would spend in a panic. He had never spent much time unaccounted for in the first place, and look what had happened. He'd found plenty of time to have an affair right under my nose. Did I really think I could prevent him from doing it again?

This was one of the few times I had been able to calm myself with rational thought, and momentarily I was pleased with my success. When he walked in a few minutes later, I asked what had delayed him. He explained and we let it go. Dinner was ready and the kids were hungry. We sat down together at the table, and conversation flowed back and forth. Everything seemed so normal. Descriptions of a newly built Lego structure by our oldest son. A brief report on activities of the day. A bit of acting up by our two younger. A request for that night's story. Could they watch a particular TV show? Don't talk with your mouth full. Sit down and eat. What was the best thing about school today? I watched it all as if it were happening to someone else. A father and his sons, eating and talking. Smiling, laughing. I was getting nauseous.

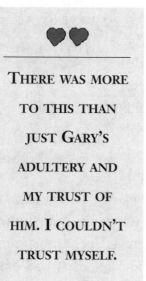

THERE WAS MORE TO THIS THAN JUST GARY'S ADULTERY AND MY TRUST OF HIM. I COULDN'T TRUST MYSELF.

After dinner, the boys went off to do chores and get ready for bed. Gary and I cleared the table together, as was our habit. He paused and looked at me, asking if I was okay. Did he think for a minute I could be okay? He said he didn't know how to help me anymore. I said I couldn't pretend we were okay. We weren't. And if I started pretending, then we would be living a lie again. And then at some later date he could again walk into my bedroom and destroy the family, destroy whatever was left of me. Well, he might walk in one more time. "But," I screamed at him, "I will not do this again. Do you hear me? I will never, ever do this again!"

So here I was again. Behind the closed door of my bedroom in agony, listening to my family, listening to the
sounds of people I couldn't feel further from if we were
separated by an ocean. *God, help me! I just can't go back to the
life we had.* It had been a lie that I thought was true! There
was more to this than just Gary's adultery and my trust of
him. I couldn't trust myself. How could we—I—possibly
slide back into being a happy little Christian family? And
yet what was the alternative? Constant upheaval? Endless
pain? *God, it feels so very hopeless. Help me to find my way back!*

THE STORY ON NEVER GOING BACK

We were extreme in our reactions to "not going back." It
took time to work all those labile emotions into a healthy
resolve of not going back to what hadn't worked for us in
the first place. Mona had to deal with the issue of what to
do with the "before" part of the marriage. Was it worthless?
Had it indeed been a farce? What was she to do with our
years of marriage before the affair? And Gary had to deal
with the issue of his dishonesty—his ability to lie convinc-
ingly, something neither of us realized he could do. And
both of us had to deal with our ability to lie to ourselves
and to discount warning signs.

So what do we mean by "never going back"? Clearly, neither one of us knew what that meant in the beginning.
Adultery recovery is overwhelming, all-consuming. It is a rare
person indeed who can think clearly in these circumstances.
The one clear thought we both had was that we were not going
to waste this opportunity to truly heal our relationship. We
both fervently agreed that we would not smooth this road over

until the foundation itself was firmly set. The "never go back" principles that follow helped us rebuild the underpinnings of our marriage, and we trust they will help you, too.

NEVER GO BACK TO BELIEVING YOU CANNOT FALL

The first thing we determined was that we would never think either one of us was above falling into adultery. Our smug belief that we had a marriage that was impenetrable by an outsider was permanently removed. What we came to understand was that no marriage is beyond penetration. The self-assurance that this was one area we could never fall into is a lie for every couple who believes it. Godly people sin. Godly people fall. Good marriages have problems. Our small group coleaders often tell the story about how they were voted "family of the year" in their home church—active leaders serving faithfully, teachers of young marrieds. The truth is that all people can fall. Given the right circumstances and the right person and the right opportunity, anyone can commit adultery.

> **GODLY PEOPLE SIN. GODLY PEOPLE FALL. GOOD MARRIAGES HAVE PROBLEMS.**

If that is true, then what can you do to be less susceptible? First and most important, you pray. Ask God to reveal truth about your marriage that you may be missing. Next, we believe you become more aware of the "right" circumstances as you keep your eyes and ears open and heed warnings that God is faithful to give us. You become more aware of the "right" person as you evaluate behaviors and attitudes expressed by yourself, your spouse, and others. And you become acutely aware of the "right" opportunities and never, ever allow them again. We'll talk more about this when we talk about hedges in chapter 10.

We also believe that once a marriage has been through an adulterous relationship, whether it be sexual or emotional, both parties in that relationship are more susceptible to fall the next time. We are not saying you will, just that you are more susceptible to the temptation. Your "oneness" has already been broken by another, and Satan can and will twist the truth, tempting you to think that since the damage has already been done, there's no harm in committing adultery again. And those thoughts will come at an opportune time, perhaps when you're feeling lonely and isolated or when you're just vulnerable and suddenly find yourself appreciated and cared for by another person. The point is, never go back to believing that you or anyone else is invulnerable to adultery.

NEVER GO BACK TO OLD HABITS

Second, we decided we would never go back to the old habits that helped us make this trip. We would develop new, healthier habits in our marriage. For example, we began to make time for each other, just to have fun together. We also set aside times to have deeper conversations about the future, our dreams and our hopes for ourselves and our family. First though, we had to identify our negative habits and eliminate them from our relationship. One habit in particular was extremely destructive. Whenever Gary felt like Mona didn't want him sexually, he would withdraw emotionally in an attempt to "give her space and opportunity to want him."

Mona would perceive his withdrawal as his not wanting her and would then withdraw herself "until he wanted her again." Of course, as time went on, we both would end up feeling increasingly unwanted by the other and hurt because of it. Every word and action seemed to underscore this belief.

Fortunately, we were able to act like adults long enough to discover what we were doing. We were in fact able to laugh at ourselves and discover new and effective ways to communicate what we were feeling and what we each wanted. We will not go back to that old habit.

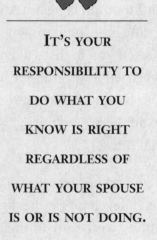

IT'S YOUR RESPONSIBILITY TO DO WHAT YOU KNOW IS RIGHT REGARDLESS OF WHAT YOUR SPOUSE IS OR IS NOT DOING.

It will take some time and energy to identify the well-worn paths in your marriage. Often the key is one partner feeling distanced from the other. When you begin to feel that way, take the initiative to talk with your spouse to see if he or she might be feeling the same way. Ask yourselves what words or actions brought on the feelings. Have you felt this way before? Were the circumstances similar? Now's the time to discover the dynamics that have possibly created a pattern in your relationship.

Once you've identified an unhealthy pattern, determine how you will counteract it. You can start by rejecting whatever works its way between you. Do you need to give up an evening out with friends or a church committee or a sports team to communicate to your spouse that he or she is the most important person on earth? Then do it! Quit saying, "If he or she will do this, I'll do that." It's your responsibility to do what you know is right regardless of what your spouse is or is not doing.

Some couples, having discovered a bad habit, have found new ways to communicate and spend time together. Some cook together, take a class together, walk together, or schedule a regular date. There are endless resources out there with thousands of ideas. The point is to identify what you need to change and then work together to make the changes.

NEVER GO BACK TO COMPLAINING

Last, we have given up on complaining—especially the most destructive form of all: nonverbal complaining. Silent complaining is what you do when you take mental note every time your spouse drops dirty clothes on the floor, doesn't brush his or her teeth, doesn't make the bed, doesn't clean the kitchen, doesn't put gas in the car—you name it. If you insist on keeping track of those pesky, irritating behaviors in your spouse, your heart will soon be filled with resentment. You may think you're being a good Christian, practically a martyr, really, for putting up with all those things, especially since you're not complaining out

IF YOU INSIST ON KEEPING TRACK OF THOSE PESKY, IRRITATING BEHAVIORS IN YOUR SPOUSE, YOUR HEART WILL SOON BE FILLED WITH RESENTMENT.

loud. After all, Proverbs 21:9 says, "Better to live on a corner of the roof than share a house with a quarrelsome wife." And you certainly don't want to be considered "quarrelsome." (By the way, the truth of this proverb remains, whether the word is *wife* or *husband*.)

If you continually complain nonverbally, however, resentment will continue to build and eventually spill out. And we tend to express resentment in ways unrelated to the original source, causing divisiveness in the same way verbal complaining does. For example, working late every evening is not the solution to your wife's talking during your favorite TV show. Likewise, slamming pans on the stove is not going to convince your husband that he needs to pick up his dirty socks! If what is bothering you is an issue, treat it as such, and deal with it constructively. If it is simply an annoyance and not worth dealing with as an issue, let it go. We all put up with some things in each other. We'll stop that in heaven, not here on earth. A marriage is not good because you're both perfect. Rather, a marriage is good because you both encourage each other to be the best man or woman God intends. Let's focus our energies on the important things.

Not going back can be hard. We will always want to take the path of least resistance. It is so much easier when things begin to feel normal again. But remember, your old "normal" way of doing things got you where you are. You will have to sacrifice some easy times to create a new normal. Perhaps you'll even find yourselves having to give more than you get in return. We remind ourselves that nothing will ever compare to the difficulty of dealing with the adultery. And nothing will compare with the blessings of a healthy marriage.

FIVE

WILLING TO ENDURE THE PAIN

Why is my pain unending
and my wound grievous and incurable?…
Therefore this is what the Lord says:
"If you repent, I will restore you."
JEREMIAH 15:18–19

MONA'S STORY

(Less than one year after revelation)

I stopped and looked into the living room. My three sons were absorbed in the afternoon's cartoons. I didn't care. There was nothing left in me to care with. I had no energy left to guide them into a more productive activity. And the mere thought of trying to convince them to join me in another activity was overwhelming. I wasn't a mother anymore. I wasn't a wife. I wasn't even sure there was anything left of the person I had once been. So I didn't say anything. I simply opened the front door and left. I had no idea where I was going or what I was doing. I just had to leave. No purse, no keys. Guess I was walking.

I turned west and walked down our road. Our road is a thoroughfare between two towns, and it's always busy, especially at that time of day. I imagined the anticipation of the people in their cars as they looked forward to being reunited with their families, to eating a warm meal together, to enjoying each other's company. I, on the other hand, walked down the road away from everything, feeling only the coolness of the evening. Not caring about dinner, my husband, or my children. I was totally numb.

HOW MUCH PAIN COULD ONE PERSON TAKE BEFORE GIVING UP TRYING TO SURVIVE?

How much pain could one person take before giving up trying to survive? How much time do you get to grieve before you're classified as emotionally disturbed? I feared I was perilously close. And I was angry! Gary and his partner had "repented and been forgiven." They could move on with their lives. Well, I couldn't! I resented the fact that I had not committed this sin, yet I still had to carry the pain. Why didn't they just run away together? By now, I could have been moving on with my life instead of being stuck. And at least I wouldn't have had to suffer in silence; everyone would know if they'd run off. Even as I thought these things, I knew the absurdity of them. We all had suffered. We all were still suffering.

But it was so unfair. No one had ever even wanted to have an affair with me! There had been no desire so strong that I had risked everything to satisfy it. Gary had risked everything and everyone for her. What had he ever risked to have me? I felt like the booby prize. Maybe I just wasn't worth having. Maybe I should just disappear.

I found myself standing at the gate of our small community cemetery. Funny, I'd never been here before. I walked in. I read the names, the dates of birth, the dates of death. Families were buried together. I wondered what traumas they had endured. What pain had they gone through? Was there anyone here that had suffered the pain of betrayal, the pain of adultery? If so, what had it done to them?

As I continued to walk around the gravesites, I began to think of my father. Fresh tears flowed now. My father had passed away a few years earlier. His ashes had been sent to his home state of Missouri, so I didn't even have a grave to go to. I thought about the man he had been: gentle, kind, and sensitive—almost too sensitive for this world. He'd been a sad man. He'd moved back to Missouri after he and my mother split up when I was sixteen, but we'd moved him back to California just a few years before his death. His health problems had become too much for my aunt to handle, so he had moved to be near his daughters. He'd had a chance to get to know his grandchildren, and we'd been able to take care of him. It had worked like a family should work. He loved Gary. "What do you think of him now, Daddy?" I asked. "I thought he loved me. Daddy, he didn't love me enough to stay faithful. Maybe he just didn't really love me." *Oh, God!* My daddy was the only man who ever truly loved me until the day he died. My daddy thought I was beautiful. No one ever thought I was beautiful but him.

I sat on a rock in the graveyard and cried out my heart to my daddy and my Lord. It somehow seemed appropriate.

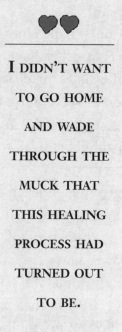

I DIDN'T WANT TO GO HOME AND WADE THROUGH THE MUCK THAT THIS HEALING PROCESS HAD TURNED OUT TO BE.

The tears ceased eventually. I didn't want to go home and wade through the muck that this healing process had turned out to be. Every time it seemed we were getting closer to being done (whatever that meant), something else would happen. I had never been so depressed. I had never experienced pain of this magnitude, and I didn't want to anymore. I didn't know if I could.

I contemplated not going home at all. How long would it be until they'd miss me? What would they do? No one knew where I was. No one even knew when I'd left. If I were ever going to be suicidal, it would have been then. But something kept me on this side of that ledge. Maybe it was seeing the pain my father had caused our family by his inability to cope with life. Maybe it was just a "God thing."

The hardness and pointed edges of the rock I was sitting on penetrated my thoughts as well as my body. It was beginning to look like rain. It was time to go. But if I went home, I would be walking back into the same house I'd left. I knew the pain that awaited me there. I knew the work that awaited both Gary and me. And I knew the only hope was to walk through this pain—me, Gary, and the Lord.

So I got up from my rock, said good-bye to my dad, and walked home with my Lord.

GARY'S STORY

(Less than six months after revelation)

Our anniversary was coming up. We had been married nineteen years. What made this one a real milestone in my opinion was the fact that it was just four months after the revelation of my affair. Four long and very painful months had gone by, and we had survived them. Mona was starting to have days without crying. They were few and far between, but we were healing, and that was important. Maybe we were through the worst of it.

SHE NEEDED A BREAK AND SO DID I.

I wanted to do something nice for our anniversary, but something expensive and crazy was just out of the question. Neither of us was really in the mood for celebrating.

We talked about it and decided we would go camping, just the two of us. We both enjoyed camping. We camped as a family for vacations, and we'd gone by ourselves before. This time we would leave the kids with grandparents and enjoy a few days of peace and quiet. She and I would pull our little home away from home high into the Sierras and get away from it all. She needed a break and so did I.

The campsite went together nicely. Amazing what you can accomplish when there are no kids underfoot. And it's pretty simple with a fully contained trailer. Our site was slightly isolated, surrounded by pine trees, just the way both of us liked it. The campground was practically empty. The month of May is pretty cold in the high Sierras, and the weather can be unpredictable, so most people wait until later in the season.

We barbequed some steaks and had a pleasant and relaxed dinner. No interruptions, no spills, no fights. We did the dishes together while listening to the radio, singing to the oldies. The outside air had a definite chill, so we stayed inside the trailer, turned on the heater, and settled in with our books. The quiet, peaceful atmosphere was soothing in the familiar comfort of our little trailer.

Well, one thing led to another, and pretty soon, there we were acting like twenty-year-olds again. Ironically enough, our sex life had actually improved since revelation. I would learn later that this was not uncommon. But at that point I really didn't understand why; I was just glad something drew us together. At least until Mona began to cry—again. Unfortunately, this was not an uncommon occurrence, either. Something triggered something, and a wave of thoughts and emotions seemed to overtake her. What would normally have been an occasion for quiet pillow talk had turned into yet another episode of my holding her while she wept.

I asked what was bothering her. Was it anything I had done or said? "No, it's nothing you did. I just can't help it."

"Is there anything I can do to help you?" I asked.

"No, just hold me."

I held her for quite a while. I was trying to be strong for her. I was trying to hold it all together for us, for our marriage, and for our family.

We talked about what it was that made her cry. For the first time she told me that sometimes pictures of my partner and me would flash through her head while we were making love, and she would just lose it. She assured me it was nothing I did.

What did she mean, nothing I did? How could she even say that? Of course it was something I did. I cheated on her! I involved another person in our private life. The man she loved without condition betrayed her. I think I had always suspected what it was that made her cry, but I'd never asked before, and right then I was sorry I had.

I had told myself all through the affair that it had nothing to do with Mona, that it was something separate from our marriage, but in fact it had everything to do with her. It could not be separated, and she would bear the brunt of my sin. She would feel the betrayal more deeply than I had ever imagined possible. She was lying there engulfed in pain of my making. And then she began apologizing to me for ruining our time together!

I couldn't take it anymore. I broke down. I lost it. I broke in a new and different way as I realized the depth of her injury.

That night I wailed as I began to understand the pain I had caused. I had cut her to her very soul. I had not known I was capable of inflicting such a wound. How could I live with this knowledge? How could she ever forgive me? I honestly didn't know how I would have reacted if the situation had been reversed. How could I even ask it of her? What kind of a man was I?

She held me and whispered it was going to be all right.

She comforted me while I began to comprehend what I had done. I lay there, overcome by the magnitude of the task I had placed before us. Forgiveness and restoration took on new meaning for me that night.

THE STORY ON ENDURING THE PAIN

Focus on the Family had a radio show in 1983 titled "Victims of Affairs." Dr. James Dobson related a story that had been told to him.

A woman grew up in the Soviet Union. In 1941, although she was not a Jew, she was put in a Nazi concentration camp until the war was over. While there she witnessed horrific beatings and killings, lost family members, and endured atrocities most of us will never know or understand. She somehow survived, came to the United States, and married. Her husband had an affair and left her for another woman. She had this to say about her experience with her husband: "That was the most painful experience of my life."

ADULTERY CAUSES PAIN. ADULTERY RECOVERY IS PAINFUL.

When we heard this story in the early stages of our recovery, we wept with relief. We were not crazy or overreacting. We were indeed experiencing the worst trauma of our lives. And it affirmed for us that there could be something even more difficult than what we were going through—to experience this without our spouse.

Adultery causes pain. Adultery recovery is painful. We believe—we know—that when we seek the Lord and walk this road of recovery with him, there is hope. But the pain remains. Life becomes a roller-coaster ride. You feel as if you have climbed that first and highest hill, dangled over the edge until you think you'll burst from the suspense, and then been propelled downward at a stomach-clenching rate of speed. All the while, you realize you have no power to control the fall. The pain accompanies you along this path, the highs and the lows. And just when you think you've reached the end of the ride, a whole new segment becomes visible. And unlike the roller-coaster ride, there is very little "thrill" to the process. Most of us fully understand those who say they would give all they have to get off this ride. It affects you physically, emotionally, and spiritually. A weariness previously unknown saps you of your strength. In this circumstance, we can come to understand Paul's words in 2 Corinthians 12:9. "But he said to me, 'My grace is sufficient for you, for my power is made perfect in weakness.'"

If there were only one thing we could say to you who are on this ride, it would be to ride it out. Complete the journey. To jump off in the middle of the ride may feel better now, but in the long run you will find yourself on another ride just as terrifying and painful.

Couples begin our support groups from many different places. Some walk in holding hands, while others seem to keep as much space between them as possible. Some appear strong and resilient; others are so fragile you wonder how they even made it to group. The one common denominator is the pain. It is expressed differently, it is responded to differently, but it is always present. We tell them that this group is not going to be fun. We tell them this is work—hard and painful work. We tell them in all likelihood they will get worse before they get better. But we tell them that it is worth it and that they can do it.

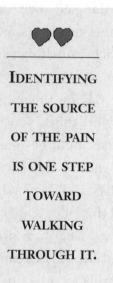

IDENTIFYING THE SOURCE OF THE PAIN IS ONE STEP TOWARD WALKING THROUGH IT.

UNDERSTAND THE SOURCES OF PAIN

As much as the presentation of pain may vary, the sources do not. We have found that identifying the source of the pain is one step toward walking through it.

The Infidel

One primary source of the pain—the infidel's behavior—seems as though it would be fairly easy to identify, yet often this is not the case. Gary's excruciating realization of the depth of damage and pain his infidelity caused came only after a few months and many different experiences. Through our groups we've come to realize that our experience was not uncommon. It is definitely a healing moment, however, when *both* can acknowledge the depth of pain the infidel has caused. Yet it is not something that can be forced. It occurs when two people share their feelings in an honest and ongoing process. One woman told us that her husband's inability or unwillingness to look at his part cost them years of pain.

The Spouse

The spouse needs to realize he or she can contribute to the pain as well. Spouses can do this in many ways. One of the most common is by whom they tell about the adultery and how they share that information. In their agitated, emotional state, spouses often confront both young and adult children, as well as friends and other family members, with facts and information they will later regret sharing. This commonly happens in the early stages after revelation.

We encourage couples to decide *together* who to tell and what to tell them. Sharing with people who will make the journey more difficult only increases the pain. Putting young children in the position of dealing with a parent's sin can be detrimental to the children's emotional or spiritual health.

> **WE ENCOURAGE COUPLES TO DECIDE *TOGETHER* WHO TO TELL AND WHAT TO TELL THEM.**

While we cannot recommend any absolutes for discussing the matter with children or relatives, the reality is that those who are told all the details about the infidelity are rarely told all the details about the restoration process as it progresses. Yet we expect them to move along the same path toward healing with only half the information. It is an unfairly placed burden on those who love us and want to protect us from harm.

Of course, those close to you will know something is wrong, but they do not need to be told details that aren't vital for them to know or that may make it difficult for them to remain neutral in their relationship with you and your spouse. Remember, you can never take back what's been said.

We're not suggesting you pretend everything is okay. In our case, our children were young, and we did not tell them specifics until we began writing this book. They knew we had problems and knew we were seeing a counselor, but they were also reassured that we were going to try to work it out. Any questions they had were answered honestly and age appropriately. Our responses didn't eliminate the pain for them, but we didn't have to do repair work later.

If you've read the preceding paragraphs with a sinking feeling, please know that it is never too late to set proper boundaries with those who have been told too much. We suggest you go as a couple and explain that you will be working together to heal your marriage. Encourage them to support both of you in a marriage crisis, not just one individual. If you need to apologize for words or an attitude, do so. Assure them that when their assistance is needed, you will come to them then. And encourage them to pray for *both* of you. Prayer is an important role anyone who loves you can play.

We also suggest to couples that they predetermine what to say to anyone who approaches them. News travels fast, especially scandalous news, so be prepared with the words you have agreed to share.

Early in our groups, we tell the couples that there are no bad guys or good guys here. There are marriages in trouble. And our role is to help the marriage survive and thrive. We encourage them to keep that same focus.

The Culture

Another source of pain is the world's view of marriage and sexuality. Our society is obsessed with sexual relationships. It pervades our newspapers, magazines, television, movies, and even radio. Common conversation between people is littered with sexual innuendo and jokes about sexual behavior and adultery. In the aftermath of revelation, the mere volume of it astonished us. How had we not comprehended the prevalence of this type of conversation? In his Word, God warns us repeatedly about keeping ourselves occupied with what is lovely and pure. We haven't done this, especially as a society. Add to that the fact that in the entertainment industry the infidel is often portrayed as the "good" character, the spouse as one deserving of the betrayal, and the pain quotient goes up. We found, and have heard from many other couples, the task of renting a movie is almost impossible. You decide to take a little time off, escape for a few hours, think about something else, laugh. We've left movie rental stores in more pain than we arrived with. And trying to find something innocuous on television was a joke.

Within two weeks of Gary's revelation, our local newspaper carried two articles on adultery. The primary message? Its prevalence and the near impossibility of saving the marriage afterward. Both articles reinforced what author Peggy Vaughn calls the "monogamy myth"—the myth that monogamy is supported by our society. Therefore, if an affair happens, it's seen strictly as a personal failure of all the people involved. A lot of people believe that. A lot of us in recovery have had to face the fact that we, too, believed it. We spent much time and energy beating ourselves up rather than working on our marriage relationship.

END PAIN IN HEALTHY WAYS

Owing to the fact that this is such a painful experience, we look for ways to escape. Much like the lancing of a boil, the touch required to drain it causes some pain, and the normal response is to pull away. It is easy to fall into thinking that if we'll just leave it alone, it will heal on its own. It feels as though what we're doing is making it worse. In the chapter on talking (chapter 7), we'll discuss more specific principles and tools. However, here we'd like to address two of the most common unhealthy attempts to end the pain.

Spare Me

First is the infidel's desire to spare the spouse more pain. A common example of this occurs when the infidel accidentally sees a former partner or is actually contacted by a former partner. The infidel withholds this information from the spouse, knowing it will hurt the spouse and precipitate another long episode of grief. Unfortunately, we have seen what happens when the information comes out later—and rest assured it will. The spouse feels he or she has once again been deceived, and has great difficulty believing the infidel didn't initiate the contact or respond inappropriately to the contact. The healing process in the marriage is set back significantly.

It is so much easier to deal with truth. And when truth is handled correctly, the infidel has some control over how the spouse is exposed to it.

Acknowledging a contact will indeed bring questions. Don't sidestep them. Be bold. Many episodes of adultery happen within the workplace, so unless the infidel or the partner has changed jobs, contacts will inevitably occur. It is best if your spouse hears this information from you. And if your spouse asks how the contact made you feel, be honest. Most spouses are not opting to stay with infidels who are devoid of emotions; therefore, an answer that denies emotions feels like a lie—again. A simple "I felt sad," "I was very uncomfortable," or "I felt guilty for just being there" followed by an affirmation that this marriage is where the infidel will be putting energy and effort reaffirms the commitment to the spouse.

The point is that one of the biggest hurts experienced by the spouse is the deception. Anything that even remotely resembles deception causes more pain. And we have heard countless times from many, many spouses that they can perceive when truth is being withheld. They may not be able to articulate what truth, may not be able to discern what is or is not going on, but they know something is up.

WE HAVE HEARD COUNTLESS TIMES FROM MANY, MANY SPOUSES THAT THEY CAN PERCEIVE WHEN TRUTH IS BEING WITHHELD.

Short Circuit

The second common dynamic we have seen is the attempt to short-circuit the healing process, thus escaping the pain. For example, let's say it's evening. Things feel almost normal at home for a change, and then the spouse brings "it" up again. More questions. You want to avoid what you know will occur if this conversation takes place, so you sabotage it by using anger, avoidance, or anything that will create a diversion. The message to the one who wants to talk is to "get over it and move on with life." This is common to the infidel, but we have also seen it with the spouse. Some spouses are more than willing to avoid any conflict. It seems they are more afraid of the truth than of the illusion of healing. Again, you may feel better momentarily, but your relief will be short lived, and healing will not be accomplished.

Avoiding the pain circumvents healing. Enduring the pain facilitates healing. If what you want is a healthy marriage, you must endure the pain. The good news is that God has promised to see us *through* the pain and to bring us out on the other side.

ACKNOWLEDGING THE LOSSES

There is a time for everything,
and a season for every activity under heaven ...
a time to search and a time to give up,
a time to keep and a time to throw away.
ECCLESIASTES 3:1, 6

GARY'S STORY

(Less than six months after revelation)

The senior pastor set me up with an accountability partner, which made sense, of course. Put the infidel with another person (of the same sex). They can build a relationship, eventually share intimate details of their lives, and ask all the hard questions. The motive was an honorable one, a biblical one.

So we met together on a regular basis. He was already a friend. We had worked together on various projects at the church. He was a deacon, but he was in uncharted territory. He would sit across the table and look at me, pause, and then ask, "Are you really living a godly life?" This man is a wonderful Christian, a servant of our God. I was blessed by his availability and willingness to help. But he really had no idea what it was like to be where I was.

I desperately wanted someone who had been there and could offer me hope—hope that I could live a godly life, hope that Mona and I could survive adultery.

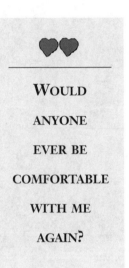

WOULD ANYONE EVER BE COMFORTABLE WITH ME AGAIN?

What Mona and I were experiencing offered very little hope. She was in self-destruct mode. I was doing everything possible to hold the family together and keep my sanity. But I was flying blind; I'd never been in this place, either. I had so many questions, but my accountability partner didn't have the answers. I could sense how uncomfortable this friend was with me now, but I didn't know what to do. Would anyone ever be comfortable with me again?

It had become increasingly obvious to me that a barrier was growing between me and many members of my church family: less eye contact, quick turns in the hallway. I was being avoided. I didn't blame them, though. I wanted to avoid me, too. I was difficult to be around. I was the infidel.

I've heard a saying that Christians are the only ones who shoot their wounded. I never would have believed that before, but I sure understand it now. It's not that they didn't care. Most just didn't know how to deal with this issue of adultery. Since I had gone to my senior pastor and confessed, the situation had gone before the deacon board. I had been removed from all "public ministry" and was under discipline. Mona and I were never told who was aware of our circumstances, but I could tell when I met up with people.

One Sunday after church I was really feeling low about how people were ignoring me, and I told Mona. She offered wisdom when she said, "You are going to have to reintroduce yourself to them. They don't know how to act around you, so they'll avoid you until you initiate contact. They need to be assured that you are the same person you were, that you intend to deal with this sin biblically."

WHERE DO YOU GO FOR SUPPORT WHEN THE BODY OF CHRIST RUNS FROM YOU?

So I went along and tried to reintroduce myself. That sometimes worked with the men, but it never worked with the women. After analyzing this, I developed a theory of my own.

The husbands don't want to be around me because I make their wives nervous.

The wives don't want me around their husbands because it scares them, as if what I did could rub off on the men.

The wives don't want me around because of what I did to Mona. They are angry with me for causing such pain.

The husbands don't want me around their wives because they don't trust me.

There you have it. No one wanted to be around me. Where do you go for support when the body of Christ runs from you? I didn't know. But I knew I was losing something

NOT ONLY HAD I LOST MY STANDING IN THE CHURCH, IT FELT LIKE I HAD LOST MY CHURCH, TOO.

valuable just as surely as I had lost Mona's trust. I didn't know how to deal with it. I didn't have the strength to deal with it. Soon my accountability partner and I quit meeting.

To preserve at least a small connection to the church, I spent the better part of that year hiding in the television broadcast booth. I'm a sound and video technician, and they needed my services. They justified allowing me to stay there by saying it wasn't a "public ministry." The bonus to me was that I didn't have to face anyone. I could get to church early and go home late. Not only had I lost my standing in the church, it felt like I had lost my church, too.

MONA'S STORY

(Less than one year after revelation)

It is such an ordinary chore: standing in my kitchen, cleaning up after breakfast, loading the dishwasher, and looking out my window. My window looks out across our street and into a field. You can see a house on either side of the field and beyond it more trees and more houses. All in all, it is a pleasant and serene view.

That morning, however, my gaze was pulled to the left of our driveway even though I didn't want to look and be reminded. Such an impersonal object, the garbage can that drew my eyes. Such a normal sight. A driveway. Rocks. A garbage can sitting to the left. *Normal. Impersonal.* Those words are no longer in my vocabulary. Nothing is normal and everything is personal. I don't know how to live anymore, to function day to day. How do you live when you're not sure there is life anymore?

Last night had started out to be such an ordinary evening. Dinner. Kids. Of course, Gary's adultery and our pain were there—that never went away—but it seemed that maybe we could find a way through this if we could just work hard enough.

Then we'd gone to bed, and the talking began. We had discussed his affair *ad nauseam*. Every question I asked only elicited an answer I'd already heard, and so I broached a new subject: his one-night stand.

> ### HOW DO YOU LIVE WHEN YOU'RE NOT SURE THERE IS LIFE ANYMORE?

I had felt sorry for her. I always knew she was a pawn in the drama of revealing Gary's sin. She was the only nonbeliever. What an example we had been! She was young, naive. I knew she wasn't innocent, but I held the rest of us as believers in Christ to a higher standard.

I had briefly met with this young woman after revelation. It had, of course, been awkward, but there had been some things that had needed to be said. They had been, and that had been the end of it.

I hadn't asked a lot of questions about that night. What more did I want to know? She knew I was out of town with the kids. She knew Gary would be home alone. She had even told him she was coming over. And she had. He'd let her in. They both knew why she was there. I never knew her motive. Gary's motive? Being pursued by a young girl. I've never been able to quite figure out what it is men see or sense when they describe a female that "oozes sexuality." I've seen many females attempt to ooze "it," but most of them look pitiful to me. I've seen many drop-dead gorgeous women, but that doesn't seem to be the "it" men see. The real mystery is the female I don't see "oozing," yet my husband and many others declare "it" is there. At any rate, that, and Gary's knowledge of what he had allowed himself to become as he continued his long-term affair, opened our front door.

And so she had come in. She made her intentions very clear. According to Gary, he protested—albeit briefly and ineffectively. And the line was crossed.

"What did you say? What did she say?" And the tears came again. The pain returned. "Why did you…?" "Why didn't…?" "Where were you?" He told me they had come into our bedroom. I made some caustic, disgusting remark about that and then suddenly realized where I was. I was in my bedroom. I was sitting on my bed, on my bedspread. Adrenaline rushed through my body. Tears flowed freely. Everything slipped away, and all I could see was my beautiful bedspread.

Suddenly I heard myself scream, and I scrambled off the bed as if it were on fire. I couldn't have been more repulsed if it had suddenly turned into a pile of writhing maggots. I was nauseous. Gary stood, a concerned and puzzled look on his face. He was unable even to speak.

But I was speaking. I was speaking for all of us. I reached out and grabbed at the loathsome bedspread. I pulled and pulled and screamed and screamed. "Get it out of here! Get it out of here!" I was shaking, crying hysterically. Gary stooped to pick up the bedspread. So many emotions crossed his face. I think he was afraid to leave me, but he was more afraid not to remove the focus of my hysteria. He walked out of the room carrying the bedspread, leaving me to cower in the corner like an abused child. He returned empty-handed and convinced me to get into bed. We once again cried ourselves to sleep.

How could that have happened only last night?

I could no longer keep my eyes from fixating on that garbage can. Our bedspread was in it, and our bedroom is devoid of a bedspread. It had been a convicting visual when I'd made the bed that morning. Something missing. Something so obvious, surely everyone would notice. I had been certain even our young sons would say something about it. Of course, they hadn't.

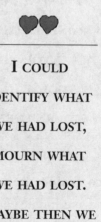

I COULD IDENTIFY WHAT WE HAD LOST, MOURN WHAT WE HAD LOST. MAYBE THEN WE COULD HEAL.

Most of what we had lost because of this sin I couldn't roll up and hysterically demand that it be removed from my presence. Even if I did begin to remove the things that had been touched, where would it end? I'd have to remove my car, my house, our business, my church—the list would go on and on. Some rare moment of sanity had convinced me not to start on this journey that could not be completed. Perhaps, instead, I could identify what we had lost, mourn what we had lost. Maybe then we could heal. Maybe then I could go shopping for a new bedspread.

The Story on Acknowledging Your Losses

The Bible tells us in Romans 6:23, "For the wages of sin is death." Adultery is sin. Adultery involves loss. Adultery brings death. But when you read the rest of that verse, you find hope. "… but the gift of God is eternal life." The point is that in spite of our sin—sin that deserves death—God offers us new life. The same is true for those recovering from adultery.

There is indeed painful loss for all involved. But we don't have to mourn forever.

There is indeed painful loss for all involved. But we don't have to mourn forever. We can move on. We can find new things to laugh about. We can rebuild something of value. But we found that not recognizing the loss, not mourning it, only made it worse. And we have seen that in others also.

It took us a while to identify the things we had lost, and even when we did, accepting that they were really gone was more difficult than we expected it would be. However, once we were able to name them, it seemed we had taken another step on the path of healing. We didn't feel so stuck.

As we've dealt with the couples in our groups, we've been

able to identify five common areas of loss after adultery. We trust that naming them will offer you hope as well as enable you to move beyond them.

The Purity of the Marriage Bed

Loss of purity may seem obvious, but believe it or not, many people miss it. In our case, we did not become believers until after we'd been married several years. We had both lived worldly lives prior to our marriage. One night soon after revelation, Mona was walking by herself and talking to God. She remembers being struck with the realization that the way she felt about the intruder Gary had allowed to mar the purity of the marriage bed could be how God felt about the behaviors Mona had allowed to mar her purity before she was married. She grieved for the first time, truly grieved her own sin and disobedience, and began to realize that impurities come in many shapes and forms.

God reserves the marriage bed for a husband and wife only. Sex is the one unique aspect reserved for the two of them. It is a picture of the intimate relationship God himself wants with us as individuals, and the desire represents his intense desire for our hearts. But just as God creates new life in old sinners, he can also create a new and pure marriage bed after adultery.

JUST AS GOD CREATES NEW LIFE IN OLD SINNERS, HE CAN ALSO CREATE A NEW AND PURE MARRIAGE BED AFTER ADULTERY.

The effect of adultery on the sexual relationship between a husband and wife following the revelation of an affair runs the gamut. Some experience a renewed vigor and desire for intimacy. Some are so estranged they wonder if they will be husband and wife in that way ever again. Whatever the initial effect, it does tend to be temporary. There is not, in our opinion, a "normal" response. The effect adultery has on your physical relationship is as individual as every marriage. We believe the physical relationship will reflect the marriage relationship overall. As you work through your issues—*if* you work through your issues—this question of sexual intimacy within your marriage can be resolved. If there were unresolved sexual issues prior to the adultery, those issues will need to be dealt with in a more intentional manner after the adultery. Fortunately, the church has begun to recognize the need for help in this area, and there are ministries with specific helps for couples.

A round, brilliant diamond has fifty-eight facets. And facets are only one of the many criteria used to determine the beauty and value of a diamond. So, too, is the sexual relationship in marriage. Love in a marriage is multifaceted. The sexual relationship is only one of the facets. We encourage you to view the sexual impact of adultery in the same way you would view the spiritual or emotional impact—as a part of the whole rather than as a complete picture.

That said, acknowledging the violation of your marriage bed is horribly painful. We found out from our experience and that of the couples in our groups that tears during intimate moments are common. This is a deep and raw wound, but it can be healed by God.

Acknowledge the violation, grieve the losses, and allow God's healing to progress on his timetable and not yours. When you need help, seek it. When your spouse needs time, grant it. When your spouse needs to grieve, allow it. Just as in every aspect of this healing process, be honest with one another, validate each other's responses, and reassure your spouse that you will be there to walk through this pain together.

> **ACKNOWLEDGE THE VIOLATION, GRIEVE THE LOSSES, AND ALLOW GOD'S HEALING TO PROGRESS ON HIS TIMETABLE AND NOT YOURS.**

FAITHFULNESS

For a lot longer than we'd like to admit, we both cringed whenever we heard the word *faithfulness*. Amazing how often it is used! Descriptions of good people often include the word *faithful*. But suddenly that word no longer applied to Gary. And that hurt both of us.

Then we looked at the definitions. Biblically, being *faithful* means "to support, to stand firm, to be certain, worthy to be believed." The dictionary states that it means "to be true in the performance of duty, vows, or the like." In truth, Gary had failed to live up to these definitions. In truth, Mona had failed to live up to these definitions, too, just in different areas.

Galatians 5:22–23 tells us that faithfulness is one of the fruits of the Holy Spirit. The clear implication is that our lives are to be characterized by this quality. We're not necessarily

> **FAITHFULNESS IS TO BE A LIFESTYLE FOR EVERY HUSBAND AND WIFE, AND PHYSICAL ADULTERY IS CERTAINLY NOT THE ONLY INDICATION THAT IT IS LACKING.**

faithful simply because we demonstrate faithfulness once or twice, now and then. Faithfulness is to be a lifestyle for every husband and wife, and physical adultery is certainly not the only indication that it is lacking.

Faithfulness can also be lost when there is an emotional affair—even when the infidel's relationship with another has not crossed into the physical. An emotional affair occurs when a spouse looks to another person to meet any needs that the husband or wife is responsible to meet. Our wedding vows essentially say that our new mate is now our number one human relationship, and whenever we displace our spouse, giving another person equal or higher priority, unfaithfulness has occurred. An emotional affair is an act of unfaithfulness.

The good news is that when those priorities are reestablished and aligned according to God's standards, faithfulness can be resumed. We had to mourn the time of Gary's unfaithfulness, but that did not mean his faithfulness to Mona or to God could not be resumed.

Now when we hear the word *faithful*, we feel a twinge. But we will not allow Satan to rob either of us of all the past or future years we were and will be faithful to one another.

TRUST

For several years, Gary had lied to Mona, and not only that, but he had gotten quite good at it. Trust is lost after the revelation of an affair—both the trust a spouse has in a mate and the trust an infidel has in himself or herself.

How does one rebuild trust in a marriage after an affair? Very slowly, as the infidel proves himself or herself trustworthy repeatedly over time. We believe trust cannot be reestablished by only one person—it requires hard work by both husband and wife. That means the infidel will have to prove himself or herself over and over again. That means the spouse will have to be open to rebuilding the trust. However, trust does not require blinders. We don't trust because we know what will or will not happen. We trust someone because we now choose to believe he or she will make the right choice.

> WE DON'T TRUST BECAUSE WE KNOW WHAT WILL OR WILL NOT HAPPEN. WE TRUST SOMEONE BECAUSE WE NOW CHOOSE TO BELIEVE HE OR SHE WILL MAKE THE RIGHT CHOICE.

What worked well for us was Gary's willingness to be accountable for all things. Mona didn't have to check on him; he initiated the contact and checked in. He avoided all situations that could have even a hint of deception, and thus Mona didn't feel a need to monitor everything he did.

The onus really seems to fall on the infidel here. This

person sets the stage and the atmosphere. If he or she is willing to be open about activities, phone calls, travel plans, and to go out of the way to include a spouse in decisions, the spouse is able to relax. When the infidel is willing to be transparent, then both husband and wife can move through the slow yet rewarding process of rebuilding trust.

THE ILLUSION OF WHO YOU BOTH ARE

Husbands and wives are often shattered after revelation because they believed they knew their spouses so well that the person could have never pulled off having an affair. Mona didn't believe Gary could lie, and she didn't believe she could be deceived.

The reality was that Gary *could* lie. In fact, he did it very well. And Mona *could* be deceived—her perception or intuition wasn't that great after all. What does that mean for the future? It means that Gary is capable of lying. When and if he chooses to, he can pull it off.

Infidels are often astounded by their own ability to lead a dual life, to separate one life from the other. They didn't even think they were capable of it. Yet the Bible says clearly that we are *all* capable of such deceit. "The heart is deceitful above all things and beyond cure. Who can understand it?" (Jeremiah 17:9). Most of us think we are better than that, and perhaps that's the greatest lie of all.

All of us acknowledge intellectually

> **THE BIBLE SAYS CLEARLY THAT WE ARE *ALL* CAPABLE OF SUCH DECEIT.**

that our lives can be changed in an instant—by a car driven a wrong way, by an illness, or by any number of things. Once a catastrophic event has actually happened, our understanding goes beyond the intellectual into the experiential. Most of us, however, don't quit living. We simply live with the knowledge that bad things can happen, and we try not to do anything to help them happen again.

The same is true of adultery. It was always a possibility. You just didn't know it. But now you do. What you've lost is your innocence. Many who work in emergency response positions know exactly what that means. Police, medics, fire-fighters, soldiers see a side of humanity—a very ugly side—most of us will never know. The loss of your innocence does not have to ruin your life. It can make you appreciate the good parts of life even more. And it can make you wiser.

Those of us who have been through adultery have seen sides of each other a lot of couples will never know. Not see-ing some of those things can be a blessing. Some of what we learned about each other is also a blessing. Mona shared ear-lier how much everyone loved Gary and thought he was so wonderful. Well, so did she. In fact, without even realizing it, she had put Gary above God in many ways. Gary was her source of comfort, strength, and affirmation. God never intended for Gary to be in that position. That was God's posi-tion. When Gary fell, he fell hard. But Mona got her priori-ties right and gained wisdom in the process. She clearly understands now that God is God, and Gary is just a man—a man she loves very much, but still just a man.

CHURCH

Most couples in our groups lost their churches. The reality is that the church is made up of people. And people are over-whelmed by the fact that anyone commits adultery, much less those professing to be Christians. And the truth is that those involved in adultery recovery do need to regroup and deal with the issues at hand. Church life cannot nor should it go on undisturbed.

We were unusual in that we stayed at our church. We simply never felt God direct us to leave. Our children were established there, and it is big enough that many people did not know our circumstances. This is not the norm, and some

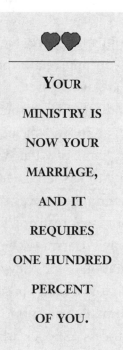

YOUR MINISTRY IS NOW YOUR MARRIAGE, AND IT REQUIRES ONE HUNDRED PERCENT OF YOU.

even advocate moving to another church, especially if the partner is in the church. However, we believe staying was the best decision for us. We would have missed multiple blessings that came from our church family.

Before the blessings, however, came two heavy losses related to our church.

First was the loss of ministry. Gary was often used on the platform for his musical and voice talents, and occasionally Mona would serve alongside him. Both of us were beginning to be more involved in leadership within our church body. It was a loss that caused sadness, but we do advocate the voluntary resigning of any church leadership position or area of public ministry. It is time to focus on you and the Lord, you and your spouse. Your ministry is now your marriage, and it requires one hundred percent of you. People who ask questions can be given a truthful answer without details, something such as, "I need to pull back and focus on my family for a while."

Does that mean you can't ever again serve in any capacity? We believe the leader you serve under should be made aware of your circumstances and should determine the process of restoring you (or not) to leadership.

The other significant loss is that of relationships within your church body. Those relationships that were mature and healthy between believers survived. Those that were the Sunday morning "How are you?" often did not. We were not ostracized or condemned to sit in the back pew, but we've had to reinvest a lot of time and energy to get back to a deep level with some. We had to recognize that they, too, really had no idea of how to handle this situation. And we've had to put forth some effort and allow some time for that broken trust to heal. Those who were unwilling to process with us were lost. To this day, some people still hold Gary at arm's length, unwilling to experience our former free flow of laughter and fellowship. The truth is, they don't want to. But another truth is that God does, and he will guide us in our church relationships as well as in our marriage.

Acknowledging the losses from adultery is painful. None of us wants to lose anything that is important to us. But only by acknowledging them can we accept them and move forward on our journey toward healing from adultery.

SEVEN

TALK, TALK, AND TALK AGAIN

> *"Do not be afraid. These are the things you are to do:*
> *Speak the truth to each other."*
> ZECHARIAH 8:15–16

MONA'S STORY

(More than one year past revelation)

It took so much to act like a normal human being. Performing the everyday activities of a woman and mother required reaching into the deep recesses of myself and dragging up whatever little bit of strength and fortitude I could find. By the time dinner and dishes were done, homework completed, and the kids settled in their rooms for the night, I was exhausted. I could relax, whatever that meant. During those days, it took everything I had just to breathe.

This "healing process" had gone on longer than I'd expected. But I couldn't pretend to be healed if I wasn't. I knew Gary was ready to be done with it. Too bad! This trip hadn't been my idea in the first place.

I did have to give Gary credit, though. He was repentant. He made himself an open book and gave me permission to ask any question. He answered a lot of questions I know he didn't want to. Certainly he tried to avoid some—especially about his feelings and thoughts. But he soon realized that if we couldn't come together now, freely and openly sharing, there was little hope we ever would.

Many people asked how I could even consider staying with him. What a question! I'm a Christian. I know what the Scriptures say about marriage. I believe God had permitted divorce for the protection of the innocent, but it is never what he wants. God hates divorce. He said so. And we have three boys. We'd had way too many opportunities to see what divorce does to the children. There was no pretending they'd be better off. But the bottom line was that Gary wanted our marriage to survive. He was willing to go through the hard work of rebuilding. How could I justify refusing even to try?

Gary came out from reading the boys a story. He'd aged a bit; I had, too. He looked tired; I did, too.

He looked at me and said, "What do you want to do?"

Poor guy. He knew what he was inviting: another talk, more agonizing, more crying. But it seemed to be all we could do. The catharsis never seemed to end.

"Let's go sit in the spa," I said. "It's such a nice night."

So we changed, grabbed a soda, and went out. The night was clear and the sky filled with stars.

We'd gotten the spa and had a gazebo built when our youngest was just a baby. It had been the first "frivolous" thing we'd ever done. But we never regretted it. Our little ones learned to swim in it, and we spent countless hours here as a family—with nothing to do but talk! I smiled as I recalled the laughter and splashing three little boys could cause in this thing. I could look over and see the pool we later added and remember times in the winter when the boys had challenged each other to jump into the cold water. I could see their little bodies running (against the rules!) toward the pool and jumping in. They'd come up screeching with the cold. But they'd stay there and swim awhile, then eventually come back shivering to the spa to get warm. Gary and I grinned at each other as we acknowledged how nuts these kids were.

But that had changed after Gary's revelation; there wasn't much laughter around here anymore. And if by chance we were able to take a break and enjoy a brief period of family time, one of the boys would act up. Satan had been having a heyday in our home.

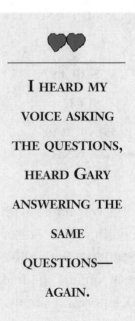

I HEARD MY VOICE ASKING THE QUESTIONS, HEARD GARY ANSWERING THE SAME QUESTIONS— AGAIN.

We sat in silence for a bit, listening to the water bubble, talking to the dog.

"How was your day?" I asked.

We went on to discuss a small problem with a client. I shared a weird phone call we'd received at the office. We talked about a note we'd received from one of the boys' teachers. It almost felt like a normal conversation for a while.

We got quiet again. *Now what?* I wondered. I could feel the emotions coming. The pain. The sadness. The tears brimming in my eyes. I heard my voice asking the questions, heard Gary answering the same questions—again. It was almost as if I were off in a corner, watching two people on a path they didn't want to be on, yet having no idea how to get off. I knew the next question before I heard it. I knew the answer before he said it. There was no satisfaction here, no new information to be had. I searched for a way to elicit new information, trying to figure out what I needed to know now.

INSIDE ME WAS SOMETHING I HADN'T FELT IN SUCH A LONG TIME.

And then a thought crossed my mind. *I don't care.* But it wasn't the *I don't care because there's nothing left in me to care with* thought. This was the *I plain don't care to know any more* thought—because I'd heard it all before. Because I was bored!

I was bored with the subject of his affair! I took a quick emotional inventory. Pain? Slight, but not consuming. Sadness? Not really. Tears? Gone. This was weird. Inside me was something I hadn't felt in such a long time. What was it? Disinterest. I simply wasn't interested anymore.

Oh, my precious Lord! What did this mean? I couldn't imagine I would ever feel this way. Would it last? I didn't care!

I interrupted him. "Gary, could we talk about something else?"

GARY'S STORY

(Less than six months after revelation)

We were in the spa doing prune duty once again. It seemed that this was the place of choice for the healing process. We could be alone, we could talk openly without fear of the boys being within earshot, and we could sit without distractions for a while. So that's what we did, turning into prunes while talking about the affair. I hated it.

I wanted to move forward, not look backward. I didn't want to remember my sin with such clarity. I didn't want Mona to be able to visualize my sin with such clarity. Talking about it, hearing the words come out of my mouth, caused her such pain. And it caused me pain, too. How could I have so deluded myself? How could I have ever thought

HERE YOU ARE TRYING TO REBUILD THE MARRIAGE, AND WITH YOUR COMPLETE HONESTY, YOU SEEM TO BE CAUSING MORE AND MORE PAIN.

an adulterous affair had nothing to do with Mona and me? Well, I knew better now. And both of us were paying for it dearly.

I lost count of how many times she had asked these same questions. And I was getting mad. I knew I didn't have any right to get mad. It was my fault we were here in the first place. But it's hard to answer a question that you know is going to blow your wife's whole world apart. Here you are trying to rebuild the marriage, and with your complete honesty, you seem to be causing more and more pain, going backward with every talk session. You know that after you answer a question for the umpteenth time, she'll be depressed and cry for days. Then when she finally starts to show signs of progress, *she'll ask the same question again!* It seemed like a sick process that repeated itself over and over.

Trying to avoid the negative cycle, I would shift into damage control mode. If we could just avoid talking, we could avoid the pain, and maybe we could get back to some sort of normalcy. Wrong! According to her, that meant I wasn't willing to talk anymore or to work on our marriage. Therefore, I must not want to stay with her. And then she would get even more depressed.

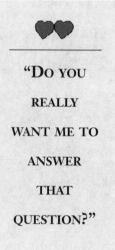

"DO YOU REALLY WANT ME TO ANSWER THAT QUESTION?"

What were we to do with this? I felt trapped and I was scared. I knew if I answered with all the details, she would go into another tailspin, and it might be days before she would be able to function again. But if I kept anything back or my answer changed in any way, she would focus on that, and the tailspin would come anyway. Plus, in her mind I would be lying again, and that would set us back even more. There was no way for me to win.

Mona started into a frenzy of questions. The answers felt like masochism and sadism both. What good was this? Mona justified her questions by saying that I had stolen from her and that she needed to know what had been taken.

It was time for me to ask the question. I don't remember how I came to this, but it seemed to help. It gave us both a chance to pause and take a breath. I looked her directly in the eyes and said, "Do you really want me to answer that question?" That stopped her. At least long enough to think about what she was truly asking.

I didn't know how to describe her these days. She was consumed—consumed with pain, consumed with questions. Some days she barely functioned. She had called me the other night, hysterical, crying about a big meeting she had forgotten, and she didn't think she could drive. She literally begged me to drive her to the meeting. Other times, however briefly, I could see the rational, confident woman I had married. This question, "Do you really want me to answer that question?" seemed occasionally to speak to that woman.

I could see her mind working, pondering the question I'd asked and the question she'd asked also. I never knew how she would respond. Sometimes, she would look at me and say, "You're right. I don't really want to know." Other times, she'd pause, think awhile, and then look at me and say, "Yes. I want the answer. I asked you because I want and need to know."

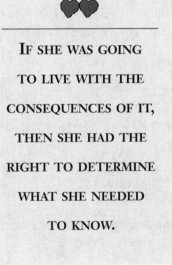

IF SHE WAS GOING TO LIVE WITH THE CONSEQUENCES OF IT, THEN SHE HAD THE RIGHT TO DETERMINE WHAT SHE NEEDED TO KNOW.

I didn't really like giving her that power. But I had to

agree that she had the right to determine what she did and did not want to hear. I hadn't asked her before bringing this sin into our home. If she was going to live with the consequences of it, then she had the right to determine what she needed to know. If we had any chance of rebuilding this marriage, there was no more room for lies or half-truths.

Then she looked at me and said, "Yes. I want the answer. I asked you because I want and need to know." And so I began to answer.

THE STORY ON TALKING

In our groups, we answer more questions related to talking during adultery recovery than any other subject. We might have thought trust or forgiveness or even sex would come up most often, but in reality, conversation is the bridge that can deliver trust, forgiveness, *and* sex.

> RIGHT NOW, YOUR MARRIAGE IS LYING IN THE DIRT, BROKEN AND BLEEDING. YOU NEED HELP IMMEDIATELY.

We also must say here that professional Christian counseling is a benefit the couple in adultery recovery cannot afford to do without. If someone you love fell out of a tree and was lying on the ground, broken and bleeding, you would get help immediately. Right now, your marriage is lying in the dirt, broken and bleeding. You need help immediately. Once you're established with a therapist, the three of you can decide how often and how long you need to meet.

What follows is not an exhaustive study of conversation. There are plenty of books devoted to communication styles and skills. We will, however, offer solutions to the most common problems we've encountered both in our groups and in our own recovery.

Just Do It

So many couples will do anything to avoid talking—and with good reason. Intense emotions, such as anger and fear, quickly boil to the surface and often spill out, making conversations exhausting and painful.

Most commonly, the infidel wishes he or she didn't have to talk about the sin anymore. He or she feels the embarrassment of repeated emotional exposure and condemnation—and to what purpose? The conversations end with the spouse being devastated, depressed, and wounded all over again. If the infidel doesn't share, however, the spouse still ends up a basket case. To the infidel, the only "benefit" of talk-

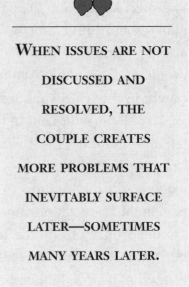

WHEN ISSUES ARE NOT DISCUSSED AND RESOLVED, THE COUPLE CREATES MORE PROBLEMS THAT INEVITABLY SURFACE LATER—SOMETIMES MANY YEARS LATER.

ing is that he or she feels worse! No wonder most infidels rapidly become unwilling to share.

On the other hand, we have occasionally seen a spouse who didn't want to talk. The spouse rationalized by saying that forgiveness is enough. Better to let sleeping dogs lie, so to speak. And the infidel was glad to comply. We've yet to see this approach help to restore a marriage permanently. When issues are not discussed and resolved, the couple creates more problems that inevitably surface later—sometimes many years later.

Sometimes an infidel balks at talking to "spare the spouse pain." On the surface, this appears to be a noble gesture. But one of the spouses in our group said it best. "Do you really think the truth can hurt any more than what I'm imagining?"

Most of us can deal with a concrete truth much better than imagining every possible scenario. Gary would often try to protect Mona from the pain talking would evoke. What he didn't realize until later was that by protecting her, he was actually hurting her more by not allowing her to process the events and emotions. Without his answers, she would get caught in the whirlwind of her own imagination.

To pull ourselves out of the cycle of talking—pain—more talking—more pain, we used the tool Gary described in his story earlier in the chapter. He would ask Mona, "Do you really want to know the answer to that?" If we were going to rebuild the relationship, Gary needed to provide Mona the opportunity to decide for herself what she did and did not want to hear, in addition to how many times she wanted to hear it. Remember, it's not over until both of you say it's over!

DEALING WITH ANGER

Unresolved anger becomes resentment. Gary had been angry with Mona for a long time before the affair, but he didn't want to upset the status quo by talking about it. His unspoken resentment provided an atmosphere conducive to an affair. How we wish now we had dealt with the issue of his anger!

There are a couple of principles that can help you deal with unresolved anger. If you disagree on what is "discussable," consult your counselor. We encourage you to seek intently to understand your motive for your position and share that with one another.

Also, there are times when it is appropriate to call a "time-out." Each party should have permission to say, "I cannot discuss this right now. We

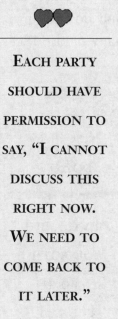

EACH PARTY SHOULD HAVE PERMISSION TO SAY, "I CANNOT DISCUSS THIS RIGHT NOW. WE NEED TO COME BACK TO IT LATER."

need to come back to it later." Indeed, this will probably not be met with great enthusiasm, but it needs to be allowed. Our greatest caution for those choosing this option is to make sure you do come back to it. Your husband or wife will be much more willing to cooperate with you on this if he or she sees you keeping your word and providing the opportunity later. And that responsibility falls to the one who called the time-out. In fact, it might be helpful to say, "I cannot discuss this right now. We need to come back to it later. Let's reconvene in an hour" (or whatever time frame seems most appropriate).

Additionally, it is important to understand that processing and venting are two different things. Venting gets it all out. Processing frequently involves venting, but the end result of processing is to let it go.

KEEP IT PRIVATE

Find private times for these discussions. As we've told you, many of our discussions occurred in the spa, where we were

NOT ONLY DO YOU NEED PRIVACY, BUT YOU BOTH NEED TO FEEL SAFE.

almost assured privacy. Most all of our couples spent many nights talking in bed. It was quiet. The other family members were asleep. The phone and doorbell didn't ring very often. The couples didn't get a lot of sleep, but they did get a lot of work done. And we believe the quietness of night helps control the volume a little, too.

Not only do you need privacy, but you both need to feel safe. You each need to speak the absolute truth "in love" from your hearts. This is not the time to minimize or criticize another's feelings or perceptions. Feelings and perceptions are real, even those we may not believe are warranted, and the goal is to help each other resolve them. Make it a point to listen carefully, and do your best to affirm your spouse. If possible, thank your husband or wife for telling you the truth. Asking to hear the truth and telling the truth are both difficult, so realize that you're both being extremely vulnerable here. In addition, these conversations must be kept between the two of you. It is difficult enough to try and work this through together without worrying about whoever else might be told. If one of you feels a need to share something your spouse has shared with you, we believe you need that spouse's permission first.

Rebuilding trust is a long process, and talking together can be the beginning—for both of you. The spouse has trust issues because of the betrayal, lies, and deception. The infidel has trust issues because he or she is now vulnerable to the spouse. The spouse is now in possession of some very effective weapons that could easily be turned against the infidel. Your commitment to each other means that you choose to use the knowledge for the good of your marriage, not for its destruction.

RESPOND TO EMOTIONAL OUTBURSTS

We would love to open this section with "*If* an emotional outburst occurs …," but we know better. "I didn't even know she knew such words!" "I've never heard him talk that way before!" "This is a person I've never met!" We've heard these statements many times in our groups, because, sadly, emotional outbursts will occur. They will not be pretty, and they shock most of us. Intellectually, we know that inside an emotional outburst is a very hurt and angry child. But the reality is that very little, if any, work can be accomplished in an atmosphere of emotional volatility. If you've

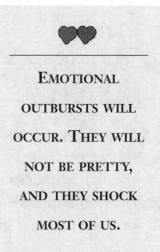

EMOTIONAL OUTBURSTS WILL OCCUR. THEY WILL NOT BE PRETTY, AND THEY SHOCK MOST OF US.

just let loose on your partner, this is a good time for you to reschedule a talk. And when you've cooled down, go to your spouse and apologize. Apologize for whatever you said or did that did not help the healing process. We don't believe you need to apologize for the feelings—those are real and true—but you do need to say you're sorry for the way you handled them at that particular moment.

For those of you on the receiving end of the emotional outburst, we encourage you not to react to it. That doesn't mean to walk away and ignore the person; we're asking you to ignore the behavior. Gary took to heart Proverbs 15:1: "A gentle answer turns away wrath, but a harsh word stirs up anger." When Mona lost it, he didn't respond in anger or even hurt. He focused on what she was feeling. He would either acknowledge the feeling ("You are in such pain") or

> THE TRUTH IS THAT NO ONE CAN CONTROL THE MANNER OR THE TIME IN WHICH ANOTHER PERSON PROCESSES ANYTHING, MUCH LESS A TRAUMATIC EVENT.

kindly share truth. ("We can't make any progress if you just scream at me. Talk to me. Explain to me. Let's work together.") It was difficult to continue an emotional outburst under those circumstances. Somewhere between his "gentle answer" and the Holy Spirit, Mona could sometimes recover her demeanor.

Responding graciously to emotional outbursts is difficult to say the least. In addition, we often see infidels do well for a while and then begin responding emotionally themselves. Many times the rationale given for this change in behavior is a desire to try to control the pain the spouse is feeling. It is as though a specific amount of processing time is allotted and anything beyond that is deemed unacceptable. Now it is time to "move on" and "quit dredging up the pain all the time." What we have observed when this occurs is that while one spouse believes he or she helping, what in fact happens is that the processing is set back significantly. The truth is that no one can control the manner or the time in which another person processes anything, much less a traumatic event. The goal is for both of you to move through it and end up with a relationship you're able to enjoy together.

Talk to one another. Keep it private. Help each other process through at your own rates and in your own ways. Focus on healing. It's worth it!

EIGHT

FORGIVENESS

"For if you forgive men when they sin against you,
your heavenly Father will also forgive you."
MATTHEW 6:14

GARY'S STORY

(Shortly after revelation)

It was one of those rare mornings that I actually had a chance to get alone with God and have some quiet time. Mona and I were still fresh in the recovery process. It had only been a few weeks since the night I'd come home and confessed my affair. Mona was spending more mornings sleeping in than not. But hey, after what I'd put her through, it seemed like the least I could do was to let her sleep in when we'd had a rough night. So I had gotten the kids up and off to school.

There I was alone with God, using daily devotional material that I was way behind on. I had missed these times with God, but then it struck me: I was feeling pretty good about my relationship with God. The sin in my life had done away with any kind of a closeness I'd felt with God. But since I had confessed it and repented, I was again sensing his presence. Today, I actually felt pretty good. I was connecting with my Lord, and it felt wonderful.

I heard the bedroom door open at the end of the hall and saw Mona walk by. She headed into the kitchen in search of her first cup of coffee. This was my wife. She looked like she had been beaten to a pulp and then left for dead. There wasn't even an attempt to muster a "Good morning." Guess I should drop the "good"; we were barely doing "morning" these days.

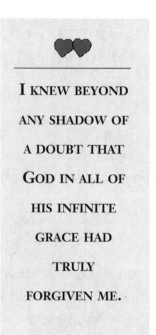

I KNEW BEYOND ANY SHADOW OF A DOUBT THAT GOD IN ALL OF HIS INFINITE GRACE HAD TRULY FORGIVEN ME.

Last night's conversation came flooding back to my mind. We'd started talking after the kids were in bed. I couldn't even remember now what we had been discussing, but I had hesitated and gotten my thoughts together prior to my answer. She had spent those same moments imagining the worst. It spiraled down from there. She had cried herself to sleep—again. I lay there awake, staring into the dark of a bedroom that seemed as cold and damp as a tomb. I wondered if this room would ever again be warmed with happiness.

I watched Mona as she successfully navigated her way to the coffeepot, poured her first cup, and returned to the bedroom. I heard the door close behind her.

I was alone again, yet I could sense the presence of God. I felt forgiven by God. I really did! I knew beyond any shadow of a doubt that God in all of his infinite grace had truly forgiven me. There was peace in that knowledge. And joy. I didn't deserve it, but it was a gift I would gratefully receive.

I also somehow knew that Mona was going to forgive me, too. I didn't know how I knew, but at that moment I was certain that she would forgive me. I knew we had turned a corner in our processing of this whole mess, and if we just stuck it out, she would not only stay with me, but also someday forgive me for what I did to her. I welled up with emotion: love and thanksgiving for God and love and thanksgiving for Mona.

> *How do I extend the very gift you offer me, to myself?*

Then the memory of Mona walking into the kitchen flashed through my brain. Mona was a basket case. Last night she once again had her heart ripped out of her chest. And I was the cause. She couldn't have gotten three hours of sleep all night. Yet here I was, welled up with emotion just knowing that God had forgiven me and that she would someday forgive me. It didn't seem right. How could she forgive me after what I'd done to her?

My prayers turned somber. *God, thank you for your amazing grace and your faithfulness to forgive. Lord, thank you for a truly loving wife. With your help, I know she will forgive me for the foul deeds I've done. But, Lord, oh Lord! How will I ever forgive myself? How do I extend the very gift you offer me, to myself?*

This was something I hadn't considered. Me forgiving me? I couldn't! I wouldn't! Since we had started on this path, I had considered what it would be like if Mona had had the affair. I'd quickly pushed those thoughts from my mind because I wasn't sure I would even want to try to rebuild if that were the case. Then I'd feel even guiltier. How could I possibly forgive myself for what I'd done? I had thought I was a better man. Mona had thought I was a better man. I had committed a terrible and destructive sin against God, my wife, everyone. Forgive myself?

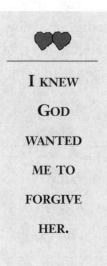

I KNEW GOD WANTED ME TO FORGIVE HER.

The wonderful feelings I had experienced just moments before were gone.

MONA'S STORY

(More than one year past revelation)

I was going to do it.

I had tried everything else I knew. Maybe this would help. I had to do something. And every Sunday was just like the one before. I determined to do better. I determined to be what I claimed to be—a Christian. I wanted to obey God in this adultery recovery process. I wanted to rebuild my marriage. And Gary and I were making progress. It wasn't fun, but it was progress.

It was here at church that I didn't seem to move forward. This was where I saw Gary's partner and her husband every

Sunday—or spent the entire morning hoping not to see them. I knew God wanted me to forgive her. I knew I wanted to do what God wanted me to do. I also knew that if we measured injuries, Gary's injury to me had been far worse than her injury to me. Why did it feel that way? I had met with her a few times. It didn't seem to help—and in fact a couple of times, I'd had to call her later and apologize for my behavior. I didn't like who I became when she was around. And it wasn't just emotions; I actually had a physical response—uncontrollable shaking, heart palpitations. It took all I had not to run away.

I told myself that unlike my relationship with Gary, his partner and I didn't have unresolved issues. I had thought we were friends, but I was wrong. She had been Gary's "friend." And to top it off, she hadn't ever seemed to want, much less need, my forgiveness. I believed that on her list of people she had wronged, I was too far down to care about. I just wasn't important enough to her.

Why couldn't I feel that way, too? Why couldn't I just not need or want her to ask for forgiveness? I knew the answer: I was being disobedient. Of course, it would have been easier to change churches, but neither Gary nor I believed that to be God's plan for us. And I assumed that was why they hadn't changed churches, either.

Now I had a problem, and I had to try something else to move me forward on this road. So I called him. I had met with everyone involved in this horror story except her husband. I dialed, terrified she would answer the phone. She didn't. He agreed to meet me for coffee at a local restaurant. I knew he was curious. So was I. I didn't know what I expected, only that I needed something to help me and that I had exhausted all other possibilities.

We sat at a table. Both of us were wary of the other. He and I had never had a problem, at least that I knew about. As couples, though, we hadn't been close.

Once we started talking, we got more comfortable with each other. We ended up sitting there for quite a long time. Questions. Answers. The conversation wandered to repentance and forgiveness. I sat there in shock as I heard him say he didn't believe Gary had truly repented or asked for forgiveness. I tried to look calm on the outside and listen, but inside my head I remembered what it had taken for Gary to call this man soon after revelation and arrange a meeting with him. I remembered praying as Gary walked out the door to one of the most difficult meetings in his life. We had discussed it at length. Her husband had every right to confront Gary. And Gary had an obligation to obey the Scripture passage that said if you have sinned against a fellow brother, you were to go to him. (See Matthew 5:23–24.) Gary had also made a couple of other attempts to facilitate healing—a phone call, a letter. Somehow this man had missed seeing Gary's heart.

And then it hit me. I knew what Gary had done. This man did not. I had not been present at the meeting, but I had read the letter. How could he have missed it? Was it possible that I was doing the same thing with "her"? Had I missed her heart?

I left that meeting with new possibilities ringing in my head. Maybe my lack of progress had more to do with me than it did with her. Maybe I was the obstacle in the way.

THE STORY ON FORGIVENESS

Opinions on forgiveness flow freely. We, like many others, had some preconceived ideas about forgiveness. And we didn't always agree. In fact, many don't agree. So what were we to do in the midst of this storm in which forgiveness was undeniably a major force?

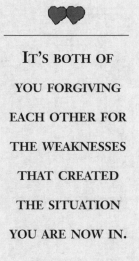

IT'S BOTH OF YOU FORGIVING EACH OTHER FOR THE WEAKNESSES THAT CREATED THE SITUATION YOU ARE NOW IN.

Forgiveness for adultery involves several things. It's not just the spouse forgiving the infidel or the spouse forgiving the partner for damages done to their families. It's also the infidel forgiving the spouse for unmet needs—real or perceived—and the infidel forgiving himself or herself for choosing adultery. It's both of you forgiving each other for the weaknesses that created the situation you are now in.

Identifying these areas takes time. Just about the time you think you've at least identified where you need to work, God graciously brings another area to light. The whole issue becomes overwhelming and confusing.

Let's sort it out by beginning with a definition of the word *forgive*. The dictionary describes it as "to cease to demand a penalty for, to cease to blame." In the Bible, the words used mean "to send away, to release or set free." To forgive is to offer a gift of grace or bestow a favor. We believe the best summary of all these definitions is as follows: *Forgiveness is letting go of the resentment for being wronged.*

> **WE STRUGGLE SOMETIMES BECAUSE WE HAVEN'T ALLOWED OURSELVES TO ACKNOWLEDGE THE INJURY.**

Charles Stanley states there are three requirements for forgiveness.

1. Acknowledge that an injury has occurred.
2. Recognize that a debt is owed.
3. Cancel the debt.

We struggle sometimes because we haven't allowed ourselves to acknowledge the injury. We think we have no right to feel the way we do. The problem is that if we never acknowledge the injury and never recognize that someone does owe us for that injury, we cannot cancel the debt. We cannot send away or release something we have never held. It's like trying to do algebra without knowing how to add and subtract.

WHAT FORGIVENESS IS NOT

Forgiveness is not containing or restraining our resentment. It is not pretending those feelings are not there. Sometimes we think good Christians don't feel pain, as if the Holy Spirit makes everything just bounce off and not penetrate. Not true.

Forgiveness is not letting someone off the moral hook. We don't ignore or disregard the wrong done. We don't say, "It wasn't that big of a deal. It didn't cause that much damage."

Forgiveness is not an excuse. It is not a suggestion that if we could truly understand the other's viewpoint, we could see he or she had no alternative. We don't say, "I understand why. It was a natural response to how you were treated."

Understanding motives and reasons can help us process, but that is not forgiveness.

Forgiveness is not forgetting or some kind of sentimental amnesia. We don't say, "I don't even think about it." God may be able to forget, but we are not God.

Finally, forgiveness is not trust. These are two separate issues. I can forgive someone for recklessly smashing my car, but that does not mean I'll hand that person the keys and put my children in the backseat. Trust requires the cooperation of more than one person. Forgiveness does not.

WHAT FORGIVENESS IS

Forgiveness is an issue between you and God. It's hard. It's against our nature. We struggle with forgiveness because the wrongs done to us by others hurt so much. We want those who hurt us to hurt like us.

It's not so much that we are *unable* to forgive, but rather we are *afraid* of what forgiveness might cost us. We do not want to be exploited or appear foolish. And forgiveness is indeed easier if someone wants to be forgiven.

Forgiveness is a big issue. If you are actively involved in this struggle, you know that. And just not thinking about the problem does not make it go away. A pastor friend once told Mona that behind most spiritual problems is a forgiveness issue. We believe that.

> IT'S NOT SO MUCH THAT WE ARE *UNABLE* TO FORGIVE, BUT RATHER WE ARE *AFRAID* OF WHAT FORGIVENESS MIGHT COST US.

So what do we do? How do we as Christians handle this big issue? How do we handle very real and tangible injuries such as adultery?

We'd like to share with you what we have learned from our study of Scripture. Irrespective of how you respond to what you learn, you will know the truth about forgiveness.

Matthew 6:9–13 contains teachings by Jesus on how to pray. He said, "This, then, is how you should pray: 'Our Father in heaven, hallowed be your name, your kingdom come, your will be done on earth as it is in heaven. Give us today our daily bread. Forgive us our debts, as we also have forgiven our debtors. And lead us not into temptation, but deliver us from the evil one.'"

We often stop there, but Jesus didn't. In verses 14–15, he explained the relationship between our forgiveness of others and his forgiveness of us. "For if you forgive men when they sin against you, your heavenly Father will also forgive you. But if you do not forgive men their sins, your Father will not forgive your sins."

Remember we said the word *forgive* in Scripture means "to send away, to release a debt"? Jesus taught that to disobey in this respect—to not forgive—is to ensure that what we need to be forgiven for—our sins—will not be sent away; they will stay with us. We'll be living with them day after day.

> **UNFORGIVENESS BLOCKS JOY AND PEACE. IT INTERFERES WITH OUR RELATIONSHIP WITH GOD.**

Who was Jesus talking to? If we go back up to Matthew 5:1, we see he was talking to his disciples. He was speaking to believers, his disciples, his children. Remember, the prayer is directed to "our Father." This is not a passage on salvation, but on living as a believer.

Unforgiveness blocks joy and peace. It interferes with our relationship with God. Could the temptation mentioned in verse 13 be to withhold forgiveness? And does doing so give Satan easier access to us? We believe it does. Christ came to reconcile us to God. He also came to reconcile us to one another.

Let's look at Matthew 18:21–35, the parable of the unmerciful servant. "Then Peter came to Jesus and asked, 'Lord, how many times shall I forgive my brother when he sins against me? Up to seven times?'"

Why do you think Peter asked that question? Throughout Scripture we see that Peter was emotional, reactive, real. He struggled with forgiveness also. Let's continue.

"Jesus answered, 'I tell you, not seven times, but seventy-seven times.'"

Do you think that was what Peter wanted to hear? He was probably hoping for something more like, "You've done enough." But Jesus had something more important to say—and as he commonly did, he used a story to illustrate a truth.

"Therefore, the kingdom of heaven is like a king who wanted to settle accounts with his servants."

What is the "kingdom of heaven"? It exists in and around our Lord and his children. The kingdom is where God is sovereign.

"As he began the settlement, a man who owed him ten thousand talents was brought to him. Since he was not able to pay, the master ordered that he and his wife and his children and all that he had be sold to repay the debt. The servant fell on his knees before him. 'Be patient with me,' he begged, 'and I will pay back everything.' The servant's master took pity on him, canceled the debt and let him go."

What the servant owed was huge. The phrase "ten thousand talents" combines the largest Greek numeral with the largest currency of the day. It would be millions of dollars to us. This was an enormous debt that the servant genuinely owed.

"But when that servant went out, he found one of his fellow servants who owed him a hundred denarii. He grabbed him and began to choke him. 'Pay back what you owe me!' he demanded. His fellow servant fell to his knees and begged him, 'Be patient with me, and I will pay you back.' But he refused. Instead, he went off and had the man thrown into prison until he could pay the debt."

Again, there is no indication that this debt was fabricated—it, too, was a real debt owed. However, this amount would be as a few dollars to us. The one who had just been graciously given mercy denied the same to another. Both of these men were guilty. Both owed a debt.

As Christians, we have been forgiven a very large debt. We are unable to comprehend the debt, much less the mercy and its cost.

"When the other servants saw what had happened, they were greatly distressed and went and told their master everything that had happened. Then the master called the servant in. 'You wicked servant,' he said, 'I canceled all that debt of yours because you begged me to. Shouldn't you have had mercy on your fellow servant just as I had on you?' In anger his master turned him over to the jailers to be tortured, until he should pay back all he owed."

What happened to this unmerciful servant? He was jailed and handed over to the jailers to be tortured.

"This is how my heavenly Father will treat each of you unless you forgive your brother from your heart."

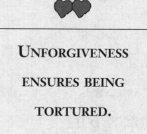

UNFORGIVENESS ENSURES BEING TORTURED.

What does that mean? Unforgiveness ensures being tortured. Think about the embittered people you know. They are even more miserable than those around them. There are tortures worse than physical ones—and Satan is king of them all.

How do we make sure this doesn't happen to us? We must forgive. So with this in mind, we offer you two reasons to forgive.

◄ Forgive to obey God.

◄ Forgive to free yourself from oppression.

We realize that we're not asking you to do an easy thing. You may be thinking, *How can I be obedient when pain and anger are all I can feel and I have every reason to feel that way? How do I forgive when nobody cares if I do or don't?*

We'd like to give you five realistic, practical things that you can do right now that will lead you toward forgiveness.

FOCUS ON YOU AND YOUR RELATIONSHIP WITH GOD

We could not forgive alone, and we have heard the same from our couples, so don't even try. Biblical forgiveness is not a human function.

You may have to begin by asking God to give you the desire to be obedient. There's no sense in pretending. He knows how you feel. Ask him to empower you to be the Christian he has called you to be. Spend time with God. Talk to him, and allow him the opportunity to talk to you. Changing your heart is his job, and he is capable of doing it.

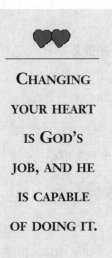

CHANGING YOUR HEART IS GOD'S JOB, AND HE IS CAPABLE OF DOING IT.

Spend time in God's Word. Look up everything you can find on forgiveness. Look in your Bible's concordance and read the verses—there are many. Read one or two at a time, and talk to him about what he has said. Ask for understanding. Repeat these truths to yourself until you recognize them as truths.

RECOGNIZE AND ACKNOWLEDGE THE HURT AND THE PAIN

An injury has occurred; denying it only gives that pain more power. If you cannot share your hurt because sharing will evoke pain, then you know it is an infected wound, painful even to the touch.

We're not talking about sharing to cause pain to the person who inflicted your pain. You need to share your pain with God alone or with a Christian counselor. The point is to identify and recognize it. Some people in pain have written down everything in vivid, horrid detail and then burned the document. The point is to clean out the wound—as if it were a pocket of infection. It must be cleaned out and treated with the balm of God's healing touch so that it can heal.

LET GO OF THE BLAME

Letting go of the blame is so difficult. We want to know why this terrible thing has happened to us. We want a reason. Blame seeks to find the culprit, to assign the role of villain. If we can just do that, then maybe we can keep it from ever happening again.

The reality is that we will never find a good enough reason for some of the wrongs done to us because there is no good reason. Stop looking! You are wasting precious time and energy. Even as we worked through our issues and circumstances, neither of us ever found the "reason" Gary chose to risk everything for an affair. He just did. If Mona had obsessed on finding the "reason" for Gary's choice, we would

THE REALITY IS THAT WE WILL NEVER FIND A GOOD ENOUGH REASON FOR SOME OF THE WRONGS DONE TO US BECAUSE THERE IS NO GOOD REASON.

have been distracted from working to rebuild our marriage. Forgiveness can begin when we stop blaming and recognize our joint participation either in the incident itself or in keeping blame alive.

SEE THE OTHER PERSON AS A PERSON OF VALUE

Every human being is precious in God's eyes. Every human being was created in God's image. Jesus died for us all, not just those we would consider "worth it."

We said that forgiveness was the real forgetting. That

means that when we look at the person who caused our pain, we do not look at a liar, cheat, or destroyer. When Mona had occasion to see Gary's partner, she had to practice reminding herself that she was looking at a woman who was loved by God, not at the woman who had an affair with her husband. It meant that when she looked at this woman, her entire estimation of her was not based only on a sin. Conference speaker and author Beth Moore says, "Forgiveness involves my handing over to God the responsibility for justice." We do not determine another person's value; God does.

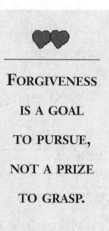

FORGIVENESS IS A GOAL TO PURSUE, NOT A PRIZE TO GRASP.

WORK TOWARD FORGIVENESS

Forgiveness is a goal to pursue, not a prize to grasp. We may repeatedly lose and gain ground. Forgiveness is hard work. We want it to be instantaneous—like microwave oatmeal. We want to make the decision and never have to deal with it again. That would be nice, but it is not reality. About the time we think we've gotten it down, we'll find ourselves in the midst of it again. Satan would love to use that against us, telling us we aren't forgiving, that we are failures as Christians. Because we're believers, he can't have us back, but he can make us miserable. Don't let the work of forgiveness detour you. You are making progress. We don't believe that is failure. We believe that is obedience. And it is worth it!

Forgiveness is a process. Forgiveness is a direction you

are taking. Forgiveness is a gift that you can give and a gift you can receive. Forgiveness is a choice—will you walk the path according to God or according to you?

FORGIVENESS IS HARD WORK.

You need God now more than at any other time in your life. Don't block your relationship with him. Don't travel this road alone. When we are obedient to God, he rewards us. Choosing this path out of obedience is a major step toward rekindling the love and trust that have been damaged. Emotions often follow our actions and come behind our obedience. Trust God. He is trustworthy.

NINE

BIBLICAL MARRIAGE

For this reason a man shall leave his father and his mother,
and be joined to his wife; and they shall become one flesh.
And the man and his wife were both naked and were not ashamed.
GENESIS 2:24–25 (NASB)

MONA'S STORY

(More than three years past revelation)

Trying to find the ten hours a week to prepare for Tuesday morning Bible study had indeed been a challenge. But I was learning so much!

I remembered back to a few months earlier when our pastor had called a meeting of all the Bible study leaders. He asked, "If you could teach anything you wanted, what would it be?" I knew exactly what I wanted, but I also knew the impossibility of it. I had an almost full-time commitment to my husband's business, and that was that. But with much encouraging, I did respond with my "want."

"If I could teach anything I wanted, it would be Kay

Arthur's *Marriage Without Regrets* from Precept Ministries International."

Even as I assured my pastor there was no way I could pull it off, he encouraged me to pray. "You never know what God will do," he said.

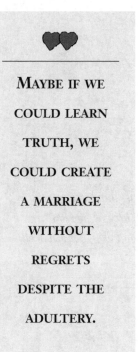

MAYBE IF WE COULD LEARN TRUTH, WE COULD CREATE A MARRIAGE WITHOUT REGRETS DESPITE THE ADULTERY.

And here I was just months later, doing exactly that. It had been a wild and crazy ride, but I had gotten permission to take Tuesday mornings off!

I wanted to know what God said about men, women, and marriage. So many people had so many different ideas of what was biblical. Gary and I had been through so much. Maybe if we could learn truth, we could create a marriage without regrets despite the adultery. And we could use the information when and if we were ever called to meet with another couple.

Our counselor had mentioned that idea a few times, and when I discussed this opportunity with him, he said, "I can't think of any better preparation."

So here I was, working on lesson 3: the "S" word—submission. I wasn't any more excited about this lesson than the other women in my class. Let's admit it! Submission is not any woman's favorite subject.

In my case, I'd spent most of my life asserting my independence. I hadn't been militant, but I had been a believer in the women's liberation movement as a young woman. After I became a Christian, I essentially avoided the subject and focused on being the Christian person I read about in Scripture. Even Christians couldn't seem to agree on what wifely submission meant. I'd heard enough sermons and Sunday school lessons to feel confident it didn't mean being a doormat, but that was about as far as I understood. Well, no escaping it now. I would learn what it meant, and I would then be accountable to God for that knowledge.

The first thing that became clear was that a wife is to be subject to her own husband—not to all men, just hers. (See Ephesians 5:22.) Now, of course, that doesn't take away from the multitude of passages directed to both men and women about submitting to authorities. But one thing was clear— when God spoke to me about wifely submission, it was in regard to Gary only. How could some people have gotten that misconstrued? It couldn't have been plainer.

I developed a love for looking up the definitions of the Hebrew and Greek words used in the Bible. It helped me understand what God was saying. And I had learned how easily we put our own definitions on to some things.

Vine's Expository Dictionary of New Testament Words said the Greek word used in the New Testament for *submission* was primarily a military term, meaning "to rank under" (*hupô*, under, *tassô*, to arrange).

Then I read what *Thayer's Greek-English Lexicon* had to say: "a Greek military term meaning 'to arrange [troop divisions] in a military fashion under the command of a leader.'" In nonmilitary use, it was "a voluntary attitude of giving in, cooperating, assuming responsibility, and carrying a burden." As I pondered those definitions and continued studying, several things became clear.

First, *submission* had been a military term. When you are in the military, you submit to the major or general because he or she is a major or general. It has nothing to do with whether or not the officer is worthy of your submission or even deserves it. When I stood before God and married Gary, I gave him the role of being my husband. This is a job description. It had nothing to do with who was better or more qualified.

Second, "submit" is an instruction directed to me—the wife. Nowhere in Scripture does it say, "Husbands, make doggone sure your wives submit to you." This was my instruction.

Third, submission is my choice! I could say yes, or I could say no. I could obey God, or I could choose not to obey God. Nobody could make me do this. It was entirely my decision. That felt freeing!

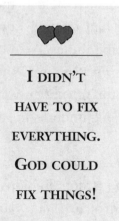

I DIDN'T HAVE TO FIX EVERYTHING. GOD COULD FIX THINGS!

Part of my problem with the whole concept of submission was that I felt I was being made to do something I didn't want to do. But now I realized that it was my choice!

Still, I had to admit there were times I thought Gary was wrong. Not only that, but some husbands out there truly don't deserve their wives' submission. What then?

At that point I saw, really saw, for

the first time, the second part of Ephesians 5:22: "Wives, submit to your husbands *as to the Lord.*" And then Colossians 3:18: "Wives, submit to your husbands, *as is fitting in the Lord.*" This was more about God and me than about Gary and me. Was God worthy of my submission? Certainly! Did I trust God to work out the details and wait when he told me to? It wasn't easy, but he certainly had been faithful through the adultery recovery. I had been incapable of trying to fix things many times, but my inability had helped me realize I didn't have to fix everything. God could fix things!

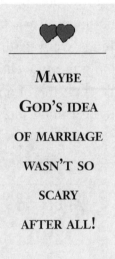

MAYBE GOD'S IDEA OF MARRIAGE WASN'T SO SCARY AFTER ALL!

Was there a time not to submit? Did I ever have an out? Sure enough, right there in Scripture. In Acts 4:19, Peter told the political leaders he must obey God rather than society. It was really that simple. If my husband wanted me to do something against God, I could not submit. My obedience to God was a higher calling. Maybe the "S" word wasn't so foul after all. Maybe I could be a submissive wife. After all, if Gary was going to be a loving husband, he would listen to and consider my opinions. And if I was truly going to be his helpmate, I had an obligation to advise him as best I could.

Maybe God's idea of marriage wasn't so scary after all!

GARY'S STORY

(More than four years past revelation)

A few years into our recovery, we had been officially released from our Christian counselor. We were terrified at the suggestion, but he felt that we were "stabilized" (whatever that meant!). He told us to call him only when we needed to, and quite frankly, we hadn't needed to for some time. Now don't get me wrong. We still had our issues. We still found ourselves in rather lengthy discussions from time to time, peeling the onion, trying to get to the heart of the matter. And we still had painful and difficult moments. But things were getting better bit by bit, and overall, we were doing pretty well.

Then the phone rang. It was our counselor. What would he be calling me for? Yes, we spent many traumatic hours together, but I hardly felt he would be calling to catch up on old times. But there we were, talking about how things were going between Mona and me. It only took a couple of exchanges, however, and the point of the call came to the foreground. He had a couple.

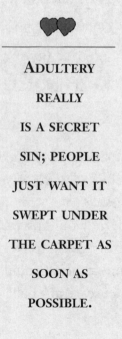

ADULTERY REALLY IS A SECRET SIN; PEOPLE JUST WANT IT SWEPT UNDER THE CARPET AS SOON AS POSSIBLE.

Then it came back to me—a conversation we had when all three of us were together in the final days of our counseling. We had discussed how God had brought us through, and how we needed to give back to couples who were themselves struggling.

One of the most vivid memories of the early stages of our recovery was Mona's intense need to speak with someone, another woman, who could honestly say she made it through the ordeal alive, intact, and happily married. I understood her desire. I wanted to meet another man who had survived and was a tangible example of God's healing power. But there was no one who would admit to going through adultery. Our pastor had tried to put someone with Mona, but the woman backed out. I can understand this. It really is a secret sin; people just want it swept under the carpet as soon as possible.

Now our counselor was asking if we were willing to meet with another couple. Would we consider sharing our experience in a support group setting? "I'll talk to Mona and get back with you," I said. I went home early that night.

We talked and talked some more. But there was really no need. We both had wanted so desperately to talk to someone when we were "fresh." Of course, we didn't want to expose ourselves, much less dredge up painful memories. We understood the desire to hide. But we knew God was calling us to give back in some small way. So we said yes.

About three weeks later, we were sitting in the counselor's outer office across from another couple. We both suspected who the other couple was and why we were all there, but we hadn't been formally introduced, so we sat and smiled at each other until our counselor appeared in the doorway.

"Have you already introduced yourselves?" he asked.

"No," we all chimed in unison. Guess none of us had figured out a polite way to ask if the others were there because of adultery!

He led us back to a small room, where he introduced us to each other. He shared some basic background and then left us. It didn't take long for one of us to admit how much we disliked being there, and that broke the ice. We talked for about an hour.

Throughout the conversation, it seemed the husband didn't want his wife more than an inch away. He was clinging to her, being very protective.

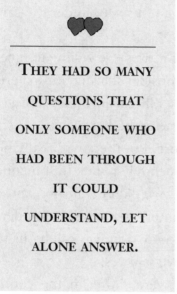

THEY HAD SO MANY QUESTIONS THAT ONLY SOMEONE WHO HAD BEEN THROUGH IT COULD UNDERSTAND, LET ALONE ANSWER.

Boy, could I understand that! It was called damage control. I really wanted to be in the middle of everything, because I never knew what might come up in a future conversation. I didn't want her to hear anything that I didn't also hear, so we could discuss it together later if it had disturbed her at all. And I never knew what was going to disturb her—a simple comment, a tone of voice, a completely unrelated story.

After the hour was up, the counselor came in and closed our time. The four of us walked out to our cars and decided that the hour just wasn't enough. So we agreed to continue our conversation at a local McDonald's.

As Mona and I drove to the appointed meeting place, we agreed that we weren't sure of exactly what this couple needed, but we sure understood the need to connect, and we were willing to be used.

The men got in line to purchase drinks, and the women went immediately to the restroom. The minute we were alone, the flurry of questions began. I would learn later the same thing happened with the women. There really was a need to talk alone—infidel to infidel, spouse to spouse. Husband to husband, wife to wife. They had so many questions that only someone who had been through it could understand, let alone answer.

I could see the hurt and sense of failure in the husband's eyes and hear it in his questions. I could feel he wanted me to come up with some sort of answer, a "silver bullet" that he could use to make everything all right in his marriage. I felt so incapable and unqualified. But God kept nudging me with a truth that had been pivotal in the beginning of Mona's and my recovery.

I always felt like I was lacking in the "spiritual leader" category for my family. And I wanted to do everything in my power to get things right. So I had started to read my Bible. (What I learned would be more fully explained later when I participated in a study from Precept Ministries International called *A Marriage Without Regrets*.)

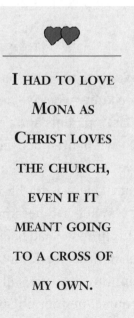

I HAD TO LOVE MONA AS CHRIST LOVES THE CHURCH, EVEN IF IT MEANT GOING TO A CROSS OF MY OWN.

The verse that really hit home was Ephesians 5:25. It seemed that many of us men liked to sit at verse 22, where Paul told wives to submit to their husbands. I guess I'd never paid a lot of attention to what he had told husbands to do. Paul commanded us to love our wives as

Christ loved the church. I suddenly realized I needed to look beyond myself and focus on her. I had never looked at marriage in that way before. I needed to love Mona as Christ loves the church—sacrificially. I needed to do whatever she needed me to do to facilitate her healing. Not when I felt like it or when she started acting like a wife and would therefore deserve it, but right here, right now. I needed to cherish and nourish her as God intended. I finally understood that if we were going to make it, I would have to do my part, whether or not she ever did hers. I needed to put it all in God's hands and be obedient to him. I had to love Mona as Christ loves the church, even if it meant going to a cross of my own.

I may be inadequate to share wisdom, but I felt confident in sharing biblical truth. And that is what I did, because that, after all, is our only hope.

THE STORY ON BIBLICAL MARRIAGE

We were not Christians when we got married, but we thought we knew what we needed to do to have a successful marriage. Gary's parents and grandparents had done it. Mona's had not. So we figured between what we had seen at home and what we "knew," we had a pretty good chance. We both agreed that marriage was for life; divorce was not an option.

When we became Christians, we learned a bit more. By this time we had been married almost eight years and realized how little we knew. Real life and children had made their imprint, but we still did not consider divorce an option. Of course, neither one of us thought adultery was going to be an option, either.

Some time after the adultery, Mona was able to teach the Precept Ministries class—*A Marriage Without Regrets*. Gary was later able to participate in the same class with a men's group. And we later co-led the class a few more times. By the time our Hope and Healing groups began, we both knew that the principles we had learned from Scripture would be essential for our couples and incorporated them into our sessions.

When these opportunities came to really study what Scripture said about men, women, and marriage, we were finally ready to listen. We had of course been exposed to these familiar passages in sermons and Sunday schools, but to see fully God's plan and purpose in marriage was significant for both of us. Many Christians can use all the right terms and quote the passages without fully grasping the concepts. What we believe about adultery recovery is that through

WHEN WE STAND AT A CROSSROADS AND WANT TO GO ONE DIRECTION MORE THAN THE OTHER, WE CAN HOLD THOSE PATHS UP AGAINST GOD'S WORD.

this process, many of us are ready, able, and willing to learn for the first time. We don't want to repeat the same mistakes that bring us to this place. We want to learn to accept and appreciate what we each have been given in our spouse.

GOD'S COMMENTARY ON MARRIAGE

God's truth does work. That should never surprise us if we're believers, but it does. The problems come when we neglect his truths and start doing what we want instead. Learning truth does not protect us from ourselves, but it does give us a place to go when we realize we've strayed. When we stand at a crossroads and want to go one direction more than the

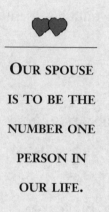

OUR SPOUSE IS TO BE THE NUMBER ONE PERSON IN OUR LIFE.

other, we can hold those paths up against God's Word. Your choice may not be easy, but we believe if you know the following principles, you'll know which way to go.

The following verses contain four biblical principles for marriage: "For this cause a man shall leave his father and his mother, and shall cleave to his wife; and they shall become one flesh. And the man and his wife were both naked and were not ashamed" (Genesis 2:24–25 NASB).

Principle 1: Leave

The Hebrew word for *leave* means "to let go, to relinquish." In Genesis 2, it refers to leaving parents. Adam didn't have any parents, so why would God say this? Because it is foundational not only for the newly married, but also for the future parents who would be letting go. God is telling us that marriage takes priority over every other human relationship. Our spouse is to be the number one person in our life. Problems occur whenever parents or adult children do not act on this truth.

Principle 2: Cleave

The Hebrew word for *cleave* means "to join, stay with, and cling to." It refers to a husband and wife. This reveals the permanence of marriage. In *A Marriage Without Regrets*,

Kay Arthur gives the illustration of a picture glued to a piece of paper. Once glued, it "cleaves." If you try to remove the picture, you will get parts of a whole. And it doesn't matter why the picture was "cleaved." It doesn't matter if it wasn't the best choice of a picture. What matters is that it is now "cleaved."

Principle 3: Become One Flesh

The Hebrew for *become one flesh* refers to bodily flesh and the sexual union of a husband and wife. It is a oneness that goes beyond the body parts and includes emotional and spiritual oneness. We are to willingly offer all of ourselves to our spouse.

The verse also says that the husband and wife "will" become one flesh. God was clearly communicating that oneness—sexual, emotional, and spiritual—is not optional.

Principle 4: Naked and Not Ashamed

The phrase "naked and not ashamed" tells us that Adam and Eve were physically unclothed and morally innocent. They were naked and not ashamed because they had nothing to be ashamed of. Neither had done anything he or she needed to keep from the other. They had no hidden agenda, no secrets. Their state implies openness in communication in addition to actions.

NONE OF US HAS DONE A REALLY GOOD JOB OF LIVING OUT THESE PRINCIPLES EVERY DAY IN OUR MARRIAGES. BUT WE CAN START NOW, RIGHT WHERE WE ARE.

Adam and Eve stood as an example of a couple fulfilling these four principles of marriage. Then they moved.

None of us has done a really good job of living out these principles every day in our marriages. But we can start now, right where we are. When faced with a decision, ask yourself if what you are about to do or say violates any of these four principles, using the following questions:

1. If I _____, will I be giving another relationship a higher priority than my marriage?
2. If I _____, will I be undermining the permanence of my marriage?
3. If I _____, will I be violating the physical, emotional, or spiritual oneness I have with my spouse?
4. If I _____, will I be able to face my spouse unashamed?

We can make a commitment to live according to these four principles in all interactions as a couple, and when we do, we will have come a long way on our journey toward a healthy, godly marriage.

Following the principles isn't always easy, and sometimes that's because men and women confuse, rebel against, or even abdicate the roles God has given them. Let's look at what the Bible has to say about our roles.

GOD'S ROLES FOR MEN AND WOMEN

What is a role? It is simply a function performed in a given situation. We expect people to perform roles all the time in their professions. If you are firefighter, we expect you to fight fires, not perform brain surgery. If you are a dentist, we expect you to fill our teeth (gently, please!), not build a house. Are we husbands and wives really so different? Can we claim the positions but not the functions as God stated them?

God's Plan for Wives

Let's look at some key verses about the role of the wife.

Ephesians 5:22 says, "Wives, submit to your husbands as to the Lord." This is the big one for most women. But as Mona shared in her story, submission is a choice, and by submitting to your husband, you are submitting to God. Now when we say it is a choice, we don't mean it is optional. If you choose not to submit, you are disobeying God's Word. However, if a wife is asked to submit to something that is against God or his Word, she is called to obey God first. We encourage you to check things out. Many beliefs we think are biblical are really traditional or cultural. Seek wise counsel on any questionable issues before you choose not to submit.

EVERY HUMAN BEING IS WORTHY OF RESPECT JUST BECAUSE WE ARE CREATED IN THE IMAGE OF GOD.

Ephesians 5:33 says, "… and the wife must respect her husband."

The word for *respect* here means "to have reverence for, to have a wholesome dread of displeasing, to marvel." This is not cowering in the corner in fear. But respect does require us to work at seeing some glasses half full instead of half empty. Every human being is worthy of respect just because we are created in the image of God. Christ died for each of us. Start there if you have to.

It's interesting that most psychologists agree that men have two basic fears—the fear of being dominated by a woman and the fear of being found inadequate. Isn't it also interesting that God's commands to a wife—submit and respect—are the remedy to these two fears?

God's Plan for Husbands

Now let's look at the role of the husband.

AGAPE LOVE DESIRES ONLY THE GOOD OF THE ONE LOVED.

Ephesians 5:25 says, "Husbands, love your wives." The Greek word for *love* here is *agapao*. This is that *agape* love we hear about in church. This love is not about feelings. It is about actions. It is unconditional; the recipient does not earn it. It keeps on loving even when the loved one is unresponsive. Agape love desires only the good of the one loved. It is the love God has for us, and we can demonstrate it only because God is in us, enabling us to love our wives in this way. It is a commitment, a high, high calling. First Corinthians 13, often called "the love chapter," is an excellent example of agape love.

Ephesians 5 expands on what it means for a husband to love his wife.

◄ "… as Christ loved the church" (v. 25). Jesus' love is a self-sacrificial love. First John 4:19 tells us Jesus loved us first. This puts the onus on the husband to love first. It is intentional.

◄ "… as their own bodies" (v. 28). Husbands are told to nourish their wives, which means to feed, support, and bring to maturity. This includes their spiritual as well as physical nourishing. The word *cherish* explains how to do this. Cherish means "to foster with tender care." It is the picture of a bird covering its young with its wings.

◄ "… as he loves himself" (v. 33). Loving your wife as yourself implies giving her needs and desires equal standing and priority with your own.

Most psychologists agree that women have one basic fear—the fear of being treated like an object. Isn't it interesting that again God's commandment to her husband counters this fear?

> **IF WE BOTH FOCUS ON BEING OBEDIENT TO WHAT GOD HAS CALLED US EACH TO BE AS A HUSBAND OR A WIFE, WE'LL HAVE A LOT LESS CONFLICT.**

The bottom line is that if we both focus on being obedient to what God has called us each to be as a husband or a wife, we'll have a lot less conflict. It's so much easier to submit to, respect, and love a submitting, respectful, and loving person.

We've presented much of what we learned as we studied the Scriptures on biblical marriage. It's a lot to think about.

But we'd like to share a couple of final thoughts that made a big impression on us.

God created us equally in many ways—in his likeness, in our responsibility for the earth, in his provision, and in our standing before him. He also created us distinctly different in more ways than the obvious physical ones.

Their Responsibilities

In Genesis 2:15–22 the creation of woman is told. We learn several things from these verses.

1. Man was told to work and care for the garden. This is provision, and it is a God-given responsibility to the man. It should not surprise us that there is a profound impact on men when they are unable to provide. One of the consequences of the fall is that a man's responsibility to provide is now difficult.

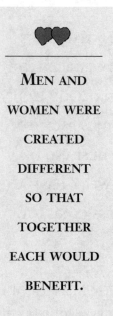

MEN AND WOMEN WERE CREATED DIFFERENT SO THAT TOGETHER EACH WOULD BENEFIT.

2. Woman was created to be a suitable helper for the man. A complementer, a completer. She supplies what he needs. Matthew Henry wrote, "Not made out of his head to top him, not out of his feet to be trampled upon by him, but out of his side to be equal with him, under his arm to be protected, and near his heart to be beloved." Woman was God's gift to man.

In our culture we often hear debates about these two responsibilities. As if one is less or more than the other. It's like the argument in Scripture about which body part is most valuable or important. The point is to work together. Men and women were created different so that together each would benefit.

Their Power Struggle

First Corinthians 11:3 tells us that God is the head of Christ as man (husband) is the head of woman (wife). This is an order that frequently causes some of us problems. Here are two things that helped us understand this passage.

1. God and Christ are equals, are they not? While Christ was on this earth, he submitted himself to the headship of God. This is not a question of who is better or more deserving but rather simply an order established by God.

2. Genesis 3:16 states the consequences of man's fall into sin. The woman was told that her desire would be for her husband and that he would rule over her. The Hebrew word for

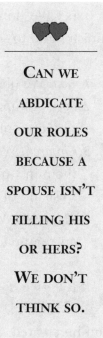

CAN WE ABDICATE OUR ROLES BECAUSE A SPOUSE ISN'T FILLING HIS OR HERS? WE DON'T THINK SO.

desire means a longing after, a running over. One accepted interpretation of this Scripture is that the woman will long for the headship order given to the man. This makes sense in light of the last part of the statement: "he will rule over you." And the Hebrew word used here for *rule* means to govern or manage, not dominate. First Peter 3:7 tells husbands to live with their wives as a weaker vessel. This was not a reflection of character, moral stamina, or mental capacity. In fact, in the culture at that time, "weaker vessels" were often containers that were more valuable and precious.

Having a better understanding of the purpose and intent of these particular Scriptures helped both of us see each other and ourselves more clearly.

Can we abdicate our roles because a spouse isn't filling his or hers? We don't think so. As Christians we are called to minister and to serve individuals in the following order:

1. *God.* We obey, serve, and worship.
2. *Spouse.* Submission, respect, and love are all acts of service—this is ministry.
3. *Children.* We minister to our children when we train them in God's ways and show them how to treat their husband or wife.
4. *The world.* We minister to the world by offering them an example of a godly marriage.

It is very easy to argue with each other, but not so easy to argue with God. His principles for marriage, for the relationship he created, are the platform he has chosen to illustrate the relationship he wants with us. Understanding this and trying to live it will improve not only your marriage but also your personal relationship with him.

TEN

HEDGES

"Therefore I will block her path with thornbushes;
I will wall her in so that she cannot find her way."
HOSEA 2:6

GARY'S STORY

(More than one year past revelation)

I was nervous. The church chairman pulled me aside on Sunday morning and requested a meeting with him and our senior pastor. Was Thursday afternoon at four okay?

"Yeah, sure," I said. I wondered what this was all about. It had been a little over a year since the adultery scandal. Mona and I were getting through each day, one moment at a time. Our counselor had just dropped us down to once a month. *Thank you, God, for small victories.* At least someone thought we were making progress.

After I told Mona about the meeting, we speculated about the possible reasons. They were most certainly *not* going to ask me to serve on any kind of board or ministry. Mona thought maybe they were just going to see how I was doing.

By Thursday afternoon I was practically dying of curiosity. What did these two church leaders want with me? I slipped into the room and saw the two of them already seated at a table. I sat down, and the church chairman began the meeting.

IT FELT GOOD TO HAVE SOMEBODY TRUST ME AGAIN.

"Gary, Pastor and I asked you to see us today because we have something important we need to talk about. It's been a year since your confession before God and the board. We have discussed your situation with the deacon board, and we unanimously agree that you have shown growth, maturity, and true repentance from your sin. We would like to officially restore you to ministry here at the church."

Relief flooded through me. A positive. Something to smile about. Progress.

I thanked them, we conversed a bit more, and then with smiles and handshakes, we rose to our feet and went our separate ways.

As I drove out of the parking lot, I felt encouraged. That good news had been delivered to me with the utmost respect and satisfaction on their part. It felt good to have somebody trust me again.

But I couldn't help but wonder, *How do they know I am actually better? How could they know?* I hadn't even been meeting regularly with the accountability partner they had put me with. I wasn't in a small group. I had no contact with any

leader outside the typical Sunday morning smile and hand-
shake. Could they know how I was truly doing with God?
They couldn't. But they thought they did. By all outward
appearances, I was doing
great! I was attending church.
Mona and I were still
together. But I was still the
same Christian guy who had
an affair with another woman
in the church for three years!
And they didn't have a clue
then, either.

> **I NEEDED TO THINK ABOUT HOW I HAD GOTTEN HERE IN THE FIRST PLACE AND WHAT EXACTLY I WAS GOING TO DO TO KEEP MYSELF FROM EVER COMING HERE AGAIN.**

Don't get me wrong. I
wasn't criticizing them. They
were just people doing the
best they could with the system they had in place. Their
hearts and intentions were
sincere. But driving away, I
realized that the system wasn't good enough. It wasn't
good enough to protect me from myself. It wasn't good
enough to ensure faithfulness. The reality was, I was right
back where I'd started in the church. Nothing had really
changed.

I realized that if there was going to be change, I would
have to do it. I couldn't rely on my church or its leadership to
do it for me. And it wasn't going to happen simply because I
wanted it to.

They were right about one thing. My relationship with God
was good. That was first and foremost. And I was diligently

working on restoring my relationship with Mona. But I knew I needed to do something intentional for myself. I needed to think about how I had gotten here in the first place and what exactly I was going to do to keep myself from ever coming here again.

LIKE PUTTING LOCKS ON AN OUTSIDE DOOR, I NEEDED TO PROVIDE MYSELF WITH SOME PROTECTION.

These were not new thoughts. But what had happened today scared me. I knew I could be driving out of this same parking lot, picking up the phone to call a mistress. I had expected to feel safer when those around me considered me "safe" again. I'd been wrong.

What little accountability had been in place for the last year was fading. My counselor was phasing us out. My church had ceased its discipline. Even Mona was beginning to relax—a little. But four years ago, I had slipped into sin subtly and slowly. It was surprising how easily it happened. At the time, I thought I was close to God, but I had fallen into Satan's snare just as easily as some dumb animal gets trapped by following its instincts.

I didn't want to be taken by surprise again. And I knew that I would again encounter times when I was vulnerable to temptation.

I thought about the men I'd known throughout my life, men who had cheated, men who had not cheated. There wasn't a huge difference between them. The men I'd known who had been unfaithful to their wives hadn't awakened one morning saying, "I think I'll ruin my marriage."

No, I needed to do some serious thinking about what Jerry Jenkins called "hedges." Like putting locks on an outside door, I needed to provide myself with some protection.

Mona's Story

(More than three years past revelation)

It had been a really nice evening. We were with two other couples, and we always did a lot of laughing when the six of us got together. Dinner had been delicious, and as usual I'd eaten way too much. I settled back into the large, soft sofa and just listened to the others banter.

I wasn't sure how the conversation had gotten there, but I realized Gary was saying something about not lunching alone with a female. One friend seemed a bit surprised by this and asked Gary what he did when business needed to be accomplished and lunch was suggested. Gary replied that he met the woman in the office or went to lunch in a group, just never him and another woman alone. And he added that it really hadn't been that big of a deal; he rarely went to lunch anyway.

Then our friend asked Gary why he did this. Now it was my turn to be surprised. This friend knew about Gary's affair. He'd watched us go through a good part of it.

Gary replied, "I don't want to be alone with another woman. I don't want to start a friendship with another woman and find myself sharing things and developing a relationship that could turn intimate. That was one of the things that started me down the path of adultery, and I never want to go there again."

"You think because you have lunch with a woman you're going to have an affair?"

"Of course not," Gary replied. "It's just a safety net I use so that I'll never be in a position again to start down that path."

PEOPLE THOUGHT THEY WERE SO ABOVE THIS THING CALLED ADULTERY. THEY THOUGHT THEY WERE STRONGER THAN THAT. GARY HAD THOUGHT THE SAME THING.

I could tell our friend thought Gary was being paranoid. I thought about every infidel we'd had in our groups. Most all the affairs had developed out of a business relationship. If not that, then it was likely a Internet chat room relationship. People thought they were so above this thing called adultery. They thought they were stronger than that. Gary had thought the same thing.

I had always had that safety net. I always avoided one-to-one social situations with other men. In a hospital setting it was easy to do. I remembered back to the early years when I had worked the swing shift with another friend. Evenings were usually the craziest shift in the ER, and this particular crew would often go out after work for pizza and sometimes even have hot tub parties at one of the doctors' houses. Well, by 11:30 at night, both our husbands were sleeping. They were not going anywhere, and by then we both had babies at home. I remembered a conversation I'd had with my friend— we agreed we would always go and leave together or not go at all. It had worked well. Neither of us had any experience with adultery; we just thought it was a wise thing to do. But several others didn't have the same agreement and didn't feel a need to.

Tonight we were with another group that didn't feel the need, either. Then our friend looked at me.

"Would you go to lunch with me?"

"No," I said with a smile.

I could see his brain working to find some way to catch me in what he considered my foolishness.

"What if I asked you to go to the mall and help me pick out a gift for my wife—would you meet with me then?"

"Gary and I would be happy to help you pick out a gift for your wife."

"You wouldn't go to the mall with me and help me pick out something for my wife?"

"Not alone. I'd go with another female friend or with Gary, and we'd all help you pick out that gift."

"I can't believe you wouldn't even go to the mall with me. It's a public place!"

How could I make him understand what we were saying? I knew we were frustrating him something awful.

"Look, you're my friend. We have good times together as couples. You and I have some great conversations. Both of us feel strongly about things. The point is that I don't want to mess that up. It's not that I think we couldn't go to the mall without having an affair—of course we could. It's not the one-time

> **I PERSONALLY DON'T THINK MEN AND WOMEN CAN HAVE INTIMATE FRIENDSHIPS WITHOUT TAKING A RISK.**

thing. It's creating a situation where you and I start to have a special bond that doesn't include our spouses. It's the 'Harry Met Sally' debate. I personally don't think men and women can have intimate friendships without taking a risk I'm unwilling to take. I know some people do, and nothing ever develops beyond that friendship. Others, though, thought the same thing and ended up with a lot more than a friendship. In my opinion, that risk is too high and the cost is too great. And quite frankly, I don't think anyone is exempt. I believe any person, given the right time, the right set of circumstances, and the right person can fall. I believed that before Gary's affair. I believe it even more now."

I could tell he wasn't convinced. The friends in that room all thought Gary and I were being overly sensitive. Well, so be it. We had seen too much. The conversation moved on without any of us changing our minds on this particular subject. Our friend still disagreed. We had shared our opinions, but what others did or did not do was between them, their spouses, and God. Being considered silly or oversensitive was a price we were willing to pay.

THE STORY ON HEDGES

Jerry Jenkins authored a book titled *Hedges Loving Your Marriage Enough to Protect It* (Moody). In it, he talked about "hedges," actions and attitudes we cultivate to protect our-selves and our marriage.

Human beings are relational. That is how God made us. But marriage is one special relationship with one special per-son. Any intrusion into that "relational space" creates an avenue for an illicit relation-ship. Often we believe that concept relates only to the sexual relationship, but sex is just one part of marriage.

Marriage is the most pri-vate, personal, deep, and thorough relationship a per-son can ever have with another person on this earth. It requires a level of physical, emotional, and spiritual inti-macy that asks much from us personally and gives more in return to us individually. This overall intimacy in marriage is what we need to protect. Setting aside a spouse and allowing another person to share spiritual or emotional intimacy can destroy a marriage as effectively as becoming sexually intimate with another person. It's just easier to pre-tend there's not a problem if it is not sexual—yet.

> **SETTING ASIDE A SPOUSE AND ALLOWING ANOTHER PERSON TO SHARE SPIRITUAL OR EMOTIONAL INTIMACY CAN DESTROY A MARRIAGE AS EFFECTIVELY AS BECOMING SEXUALLY INTIMATE WITH ANOTHER PERSON.**

The sad fact is that very few of us start out to disrupt marital intimacy. Sometimes we simply fail to establish it.

Sometimes we fail to maintain it. More often we fail to protect it. "It just happened" is a common explanation for
adultery. When we have unresolved issues in the marriage,
we make it easier to "just happen," and when we don't
have appropriate hedges in place, we invite it to happen.
This is especially true in our current American culture. We
don't have the traditional societal barriers to male-female
friendships and interactions. Although these changes have
broadened our personal opportunities and enabled us to
enjoy a great many more diverse experiences, they have
also increased our need for hedges.

We'd like to share with you two essential principles that
we believe are invaluable to protecting your marriage.

ADMIT YOU ARE VULNERABLE

You are not stronger than anyone else. You are a person, and
people get attracted to each other—we're supposed to. It's not
a switch you can turn off after the
wedding ceremony.

> **DON'T**
> **DENY AN**
> **ATTRACTION.**
> **ADMIT IT**
> **TO YOURSELF**
> **AND THEN**
> **RUN!**

Mona worked in an office about
two years into our marriage.
Suddenly she found herself looking
forward to one particular man's daily
check-in. She would be waiting for
him when he came. One day, when
she found herself in the bathroom
primping, she realized what was
going on. She had a crush! She was
acting like a sixteen-year-old school-
girl. Fortunately, the gentleman
never responded to her unspoken

cues, and she got over her crush. But she had to do some serious thinking about just what was going on emotionally and what she would do in the future if she found herself attracted to another man.

Don't deny an attraction. Admit it to yourself and then run! In fact, we are told in 1 Corinthians 6:18 to "flee from sexual immorality." That word *flee* means to seek safety by flight, to escape. We don't run from something we do not believe can hurt us. Attractions happen, and they can hurt us if we don't run.

Most counselors agree on a definite turning point in an illicit relationship. It's when the two people involved admit to each other their attraction and vow to fight it. That very act proves to be almost inflaming. Therefore, we do not advise admitting the attraction to the one you are attracted to. Rather, admit it to yourself—and then run!

ESTABLISH YOUR HEDGES BEFORE YOU NEED THEM

You have to admit your vulnerability before you can recognize the need for protective measures. Safety glasses were created because someone got hurt. Don't let that someone be you or your spouse.

There are three definite areas that need "hedging" as we seek to protect our marriages.

The Eyes

With our eyes we illuminate the objects of our desires. Keep your eyes where they belong. Appreciating

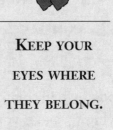

KEEP YOUR EYES WHERE THEY BELONG.

beauty is a natural response to visual stimuli, whether it's a sunset or a gorgeous human being. The difference lies in how long we allow ourselves to focus and what we focus on. Jesus said in Matthew 5:28, "Anyone who looks at a woman lustfully has already committed adultery with her in his heart." The word *looks* means to keep on looking. It stresses continuous or repeated action. Appreciating an attribute of another person is fine, but make it brief, and then move on.

The Actions

James 1:14–15 tells us, "But each one is tempted when, by his own evil desire, he is dragged away and enticed. Then, after desire has conceived, it gives birth to sin; and sin, when it is full-grown, gives birth to death." Desire is "conceived" when we help it happen, when we take things and put them together. When we add our hands or our voice to a desire, we move down that path of temptation. Some of us are touchers by nature. Some of us are complimenters. We need to be aware of whom we're hugging, how and why we're touching, and

WE NEED TO BE AWARE OF WHOM WE'RE HUGGING, HOW AND WHY WE'RE TOUCHING, AND UNDER WHAT CIRCUMSTANCES WE'RE COMPLIMENTING.

under what circumstances we're complimenting. Are you trying to make yourself attractive to another? If so, you're flirting, and it isn't always harmless. Do you look forward to interactions with a particular person of the opposite sex? Be wary. Are you sensing someone else is a little too "friendly"? Trust your instincts and be cautious.

To avoid being misunderstood and to maintain appropriate emotional and physical distance, some suggest complimenting the tangible, such as hair or clothing, and not the person. Some suggest limiting embraces to a special few and only in the presence of others. There are many ways to express warmth and kindness or respect and admiration without crossing boundaries. Identify the ways that are safest, and stick to them.

WHEN WE DAYDREAM ABOUT A PERSON OF THE OPPOSITE SEX WHO IS NOT OUR SPOUSE, THAT IS SIN.

The Mind

Sin is born in the mind. When we daydream about a person of the opposite sex who is not our spouse, that is sin. When we "innocently" facilitate arrangements to be with someone else, we're already in trouble. Rationalizing your thoughts about another person is deluding yourself. If you find yourself fantasizing or manipulating events, it is time to do a very fast U-turn.

That same mind that leads us down the road of sin can lead us back to God and our spouse. Daydream about your spouse. Remember your wedding vows. Is there something you can do today, this week, to remind your spouse of the intimate relationship you're called to have together? Daydream about what attracted you to your spouse in the first place. Focus on what is beautiful in him or her.

If you find these exercises difficult, maybe it's time to sit your spouse down and have a much-needed conversation. Don't let your marriage slide away because of neglect. Spend time with the person you committed to love in a marriage. You both entered the relationship hoping to have a love that would last a lifetime. Don't be afraid to work on it when it needs some attention. Some of us have gotten the idea that if love takes work, then it must not be real, and it's certainly not romantic. That is a lie. All relationships require energy and effort. Romance comes when you provide the environment for romance.

Are hedges really necessary? Isn't setting them up a little like running scared? We would answer yes to both questions. With more than fifty percent of marriages—an even higher percentage of "Christian" marriages—ending in divorce and a society running rampant with sexual immorality, scared is a pretty good thing to be. If you let your guard down, if you don't remind yourself that you made a vow before God and friends and family, if you don't set up hedges for your eyes, hands, and voice, and let your mind and emotions go their own way, you run a high risk of becoming a statistic.

On the other hand, you can learn from your mistakes. You can incorporate some protective measures into your life. Then maybe you and your spouse can become members of a much smaller demographic: those marriages that not only survived infidelity but also fully healed and remain a relationship both of you will cherish forever.

AFTERWORD:
A Personal Letter to You from Gary

Dear Reader,

I've just finished my quiet time. Today my devotional time centered on giving to others in need. The verse was Matthew 25:32, where Jesus divided the sheep and the goats. "All the nations will be gathered before him, and he will separate the people one from another as a shepherd separates the sheep from the goats."

All the nations will be gathered before Jesus as he sits on his throne in heavenly glory. Then will come the great division. Those to his right, blessed by his Father, will be summoned to take their inheritance—the kingdom prepared for them since the creation of the world. For when he was hungry, they gave him something to eat. When he was thirsty, when he was a stranger, when he needed clothes, when he was sick, when he was in prison, they were there, meeting his needs. Those to the right of Jesus were there to help and bring comfort to those brothers (and sisters) of his.

But what of those to his left? The goats. I can imagine them standing there with puzzled looks on their faces. "When were you there, Lord? When did you come to us hungry, thirsty, a stranger, needing clothes, sick, and in prison? When, Lord?" Jesus' answer pierces my heart just as much today as it did the first time I read it so many years ago. "He will reply, 'I tell you the truth, whatever you did not do for one of the least of these, you did not do for me'" (Matthew 25:45).

I remember the early days of our recovery. Mona literally was screaming for someone who had made it, someone she could sit and talk with and relate to, someone who could honestly tell her that this seemingly impossible task of healing could be done. I remember sitting in the dark, holding her, trying to reassure her that everything would work out. But how could I know? I, too, needed someone with experience to talk to. Our Christian counselor was great, but he was getting paid to help us. I needed a Paul to help this Timothy get through the really tough times. Someone who had done it before me. Someone who could say, "I know," because he really did know!

Don't get me wrong, God was truly the center of our focus, but someone with skin on was a deep felt need for both Mona and me in those dark and lonely times. But the hard cold truth was that we could find no one.

This is the very reason I feel so compelled to write this letter to you. If you hear anything from the pages of this book, I want you to hear this: *We are here for you!*

If I have taken anything away from this adultery recovery process, it is the desperate crying need for people like you and me to have other people to lean on in the Lord. Why not? Alcoholics, drug addicts—you name the problem—have a support group of some kind. So why isn't the body of Christ supporting those in recovery from such a dark and ugly sin? Maybe that's just the point. I believe the church wants to pretend it doesn't exist, and so would we.

Marital love is a tangible picture of the relationship God wants with each one of us, the "great romance." To realize that we have perverted the purest intimacy God provides on this earth is to begin to comprehend the depth of the pain we've caused the Lord and ourselves.

I've heard it said that sexual sin is a rape of the Holy Spirit, who lives in each believer. Most of us do not want to believe we are capable of such things. Well, we are. It does happen, and Satan is there, fully armed to persuade us that there is no hope for this particular sin.

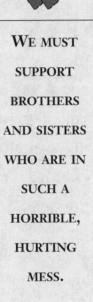

WE MUST SUPPORT BROTHERS AND SISTERS WHO ARE IN SUCH A HORRIBLE, HURTING MESS.

But God is there, too. And he is capable of healing even this. We must support brothers and sisters who are in such a horrible, hurting mess.

I remember all too well the time our Christian counselor asked if we remembered back in the beginning how much we needed another couple to talk to. We both emphatically agreed. Then he asked, "Are you ready to be that couple for someone else?" Boy, that one stopped us dead in our tracks. To be that couple for someone else meant admitting we had been there, too. It meant removing the privacy curtains we had in place to protect what we had saved. It meant reopening some of our wounds, and we feared what that could mean to us. But after long hours of discussion and prayer, Mona and I came to this conclusion: No, we really don't want to do this, but if this is God's will, then we will be there for the people in need whom he puts in our path. We'll be there to deliver his message that says, "Yes, you can heal!" We'll be there to show a way to the hope and healing that come through Jesus Christ when you lay it all at his feet and allow him to lead you through.

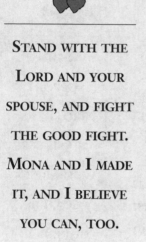

STAND WITH THE LORD AND YOUR SPOUSE, AND FIGHT THE GOOD FIGHT. MONA AND I MADE IT, AND I BELIEVE YOU CAN, TOO.

Of course, this is not feasible for most of you now. You are way too fresh in this process. But down the road, when the Lord prompts you, do me a favor, will you? Consider being that couple for someone else. It is so important to let God use what he has brought us through to help others. Think of how you are feeling right now. Consider it when the opportunity comes. Work diligently now so that when and if he calls you, you will be ready. You will have something to offer his children.

When the world would have you believe that there is no hope, that your marriage can never make it, be God's audible voice. When your Christian friends advise you to hang it up ("After all, it is adultery and Scripture releases you"), add to that advice the whole context of Scripture.

I will stand ashamed of what I did, but never ashamed of what I personally saw Jesus do in our relationship. His work is nothing short of miraculous. I stand in testimony of two people broken and bleeding, on the brink of another divorce statistic in the church. I stand here today saying that if you keep your eyes on Jesus and his teachings, trust him with everything—not just what you're comfortable with, but with all you are and all your spouse is, your marriage, your lives, and everything—then he will honor you for your obedience. Because you see, God hates divorce. Don't take the easy way out. Stand with the Lord and your spouse, and fight the good fight. Mona and I made it, and I believe you can, too.

I can honestly say, as I look across the laptop screen at my wife of thirty years, I love her more today than I ever have. We've shared our story to illustrate the reality of the journey and the reality that it can be completed. We are completely healed. We again have love and trust in our marriage. Our journey as husband and wife is not over, and it was not irrevocably ruined by this sin. God offers you and your spouse the same opportunity.

God brings us through adversity to make us into the people he wants us to be, but we must do our part, and that is to obey. Be obedient to his leading, and let him do the rest. God will give you the wisdom and the strength to complete your journey.

May he bless you and keep you.

GARY
October 2004
(Twelve years past revelation)

Gary and Mona can be reached at www.hopeandhealing.us

READERS' GUIDE

*For Personal Reflection
or Group Discussion*

READERS' GUIDE

Mona and Gary shared a number of personal experiences and thoughts in this book. Quite a bit of what they discovered will apply to you and/or people you know, because all marriages require work to become the best they can be. As you read the following questions, think carefully about your marriage. Since no couple's experiences will be exactly like another couple's, you may need to tailor a question to make it even more relevant to your particular situation and/or the unique needs of your group.

Consider these questions to be a guide, a tool to assist you in exploring biblical principles, reflecting on personal issues, and discussing what you've read with a group and/or your spouse. Perhaps some questions will be difficult to answer because of where you are in your journey, or what other couples are experiencing. If so, feel free to skip them and return to them later—on your own or as a group.

If you discuss these questions in a small-group environment, recognize the importance of "going deeper" when you can, yet you'll need to discover how much you should say about yourself and/or your spouse. This will be especially true if you and/or others in your group are recovering from adultery. Some couples may be able to share quite openly; others may need to hold back and discuss some things in a more private setting—perhaps with their spouses. That's why some questions require less vulnerability than others.

So approach these questions with enthusiasm, hope, and also the recognition that some questions may strike a deep chord from time to time. Emotions may be raw and tumble out, for instance. Anger may surface, as may sorrow and other deep emotions. Be flexible and allow people, when circumstances permit, to be vulnerable. And, whenever possible, be vulnerable yourself. Above all, honor, trust, and avoid making critical judgments of others. Now is a time for reflecting and healing. Yes, sometimes a gentle "push" may be appropriate. Sometimes, however, only a trained Christian counselor can—and should—help someone process certain deeply personal issues related to adultery.

Always start your discussions with prayer, asking God to guide you, to protect your hearts and minds, to make his presence known to you, and to fill you with his love. Only he can do the ultimate healing work in each of us. His promises are true, and he will meet our deepest needs. He longs for our trust and love.

May God bless you in your journey and as you choose to help your spouse and/or others process the material in this book.

CHAPTER 1

1. Why do you think Mona emphasized her *commitment* to God as she described part of her spiritual journey? Why wasn't divorce an "option" for her?

2. What did you think of Mona's "pride-related" reasons for staying with Gary?

3. Why do extramarital affairs occur in "happy marriages"?

4. What kind of confusion did Mona face as she processed Gary's adultery? How might she have faced things differently if she had a friend to whom she could turn?

5. Why do you think Mona's anger increased during the months after Gary told her about his sexual sins?

6. When Gary mentioned doing the marriage recovery work in God's strength and not his own, what did he mean?

7. What does an "environment for marriage healing" look like? What are some of its characteristics? Its benefits?

8. Why is it so dangerous for a couple who have accomplished lots of rebuilding to stop working on their marriage?

9. Read Psalm 86:10–11. How can we learn God's way? What is an "undivided heart"?

CHAPTER 2

1. Why was it important for the young engineer to confront Gary?

2. As Mona's heart was breaking, how much support did she feel from other people in the church? Why? What role can other Christians play in the lives of spouses struggling to save their marriages?

3. The authors wrote about having "faith that [God] is who he says he is and can do what he says he'll do." Why is this focus so important?

4. What happens when we gain comfort, love, and strength from our spouses rather than from God? What should we expect to receive from our spouses?

5. Share, if you feel comfortable doing so, a time in your life that relates to 2 Corinthians 12:9.

6. Is your relationship with God the only truly secure relationship you'll ever have? Why or why not?

7. Read 2 Corinthians 1:3–4. If God comforts us, does our pain go away? Explain your answer.

8. Why, after God forgives our sins, do we still have to deal with sin's consequences?

CHAPTER 3

1. What does Psalm 145:18 reveal?

2. How should Christians respond to a couple who are facing a situation like the one Gary and Mona faced?

3. Mona described herself as "dying" inside. What did she mean? Why did she find herself critiquing her imperfections?

4. What standard does God give us concerning forgiveness? (See Ephesians 4:31–32.)

5. What role did anger play in Gary's adultery? Why was it so important for him to admit his anger later?

6. What are the benefits, and potential risks, of both spouses being willing to discuss difficult issues, such as admitting ways in which each of them has contributed unhealthy things to their marriage? Of beginning to address their significant hurts?

7. What is involved in really "listening" to what our spouses are thinking and feeling? How can we avoid getting defensive when our spouses point out our weaknesses and faults?

8. What hope can every married couple find in Psalm 32:8?

CHAPTER 4

1. Why is honesty so important between spouses struggling to heal from adultery? Why is the truth so difficult to hear sometimes?

2. What kinds of emotions was Mona feeling? Why didn't she want to go back to the way things were in her marriage before Gary told her about his adultery?

3. When a married couple stop "pretending," why do they often face great challenges in their relationship?

4. The authors used the term "all-consuming" to describe their work of putting their marriage back together. Why does this work require so much effort and time?

5. Do you agree that anyone can "fall into adultery"? Why or why not? What kinds of things might cause a spouse to be vulnerable to an adulterous relationship?

6. Which kinds of things pull you toward your spouse? Cause you to pull away? What can you do together to increase your communication—and just have fun together?

7. Read Hebrews 12:1–13. What does this passage reveal about the following: Who is to be our focus? Why does God discipline us? What is involved in submitting to God?

CHAPTER 5

1. Why do you think Mona had to "suffer in silence" for quite a while after Gary told her about his adultery?

2. What are some of the emotions a betrayed spouse has to process? Why is this processing so necessary?

3. When Gary finally realized how much pain he had caused Mona, how did he respond? How important is this recognition by the infidel to the healing process?

4. Why do people doing adultery recovery express their pain in different ways? What are some ways in which one spouse can help the other spouse endure this pain?

5. What cautions did the authors offer concerning who to tell about the adultery—and how much to tell them?

6. How has our society's obsession with sexual relationships affected social acceptance of adultery?

7. What happens if both spouses try to ignore their pain without facing it and simply minimize their conflict? Why is it important for both partners to go through the pain of recovery? To what degree do you think they should share their pain with one another?

8. Why is it so damaging when the infidel withholds information from his or her spouse about a current contact with the former partner? In this context, what kinds of things could be considered deception? What are some other ways in which a spouse can make the pain worse for his or her spouse?

9. What does Psalm 40:1–3 reveal about God and what he longs to do in our lives?

Chapter 6

1. Why do some Christians "shoot their wounded"? When hurting people need the body of Christ most, why does the body often run the other way?

2. Do you think it was wise for Mona to wait so long to ask Gary about his one-night stand? Explain your answer.

3. Why did Mona throw away their bedspread? What did it represent?

4. What hope does Romans 6:23 bring to all of us?

5. "We found that not recognizing the loss, not mourning it, only made it worse." What did it mean for Gary and Mona to mourn what they had lost?

6. Describe the losses that adultery creates in the following:
   ◀ The couple's sexual intimacy

   ◀ The foundation of faithfulness

   ◀ Trust between spouses

   ◀ The perception of what the infidel spouse is like

   ◀ The church the couple attends

7. What is your definition of *trust*? How can a couple involved in adultery recovery reestablish trust?

8. Which losses faced by the infidel may be permanent? Which losses faced by the infidel's spouse may be permanent?

9. When should a couple in adultery recovery think about changing churches? If the couple remains in the same church, what long-term consequences might they face? Why?

10. Read Psalm 42:11. What does it mean, in practical terms, to "put your hope in God"?

CHAPTER 7

1. Mona described Gary as being "repentant." What is *repentance*, and what is involved in true repentance?

2. What effect did Gary's commitment to rebuilding the marriage have on Mona? Why?

3. In this chapter, as in others, it's clear that Mona needed to ask Gary the same questions, over and over. Why do you think this was an important part of her healing process?

4. Why did Gary feel trapped in the "question cycle," thinking that no matter how he'd answer, the results would cause Mona to go into a tailspin? Should there be limits to the type of questions the spouse asks the infidel? Why or why not?

5. Why do you think a "typical" infidel doesn't want to talk?

6. Why do you think Mona was surprised when she no longer needed to talk with Gary about his affair?

7. When during a conversation is a "time-out" appropriate? Who should resume the talk after a time-out? Why?

8. Why is quiet, private discussion time essential to healing?

9. What are some guidelines for managing emotional outbursts during painful discussions?

Chapter 8

1. How does spending time alone with God help us keep our defenses up so we can stand firm when temptations come?

2. What does the word *forgiveness* mean? Define what forgiveness is, and what it isn't, according to the Bible.

3. What role do you think forgiveness—God's forgiveness of us, our forgiveness of others—plays during the process of healing from the wounds of adultery?

4. Why can it be so hard for us to forgive ourselves after we've sinned? What obstacles can stand in the way of forgiving a spouse? What does Ephesians 4:29–32 say about this?

5. If you were Mona, how would you have responded when Gary's former partner didn't need or want Mona's forgiveness?

6. The authors believe forgiveness for adultery should also include the infidel's forgiveness of the spouse for unmet needs—real or perceived. What do you think about this?

7. What happens when we don't allow ourselves to acknowledge how other people have injured us? What effect does that have on our ability to forgive?

8. What kinds of things make us afraid to forgive? Why it is important to ask God to give us the desire to obey him by forgiving ourselves and others, instead of waiting for our emotions to make us willing to forgive?

9. What did you think about as you read Matthew 6:9–15? List some consequences of unforgiveness. Why, in light of this, do people choose not to forgive?

10. "Forgiveness," the authors wrote, "is a goal to pursue, not a prize to grasp." Discuss what this means.

11. What steps can a couple take to help one another on the path toward forgiveness?

CHAPTER 9

1. As you read the meanings of *submission*, what did you think about? How did you feel?

2. What does the phrase "as to the Lord" in Ephesians 5:22 mean? What does it reveal about God's role?

3. How might all of us, as the body of Christ, benefit when we allow God to use the lessons we've learned to help others?

4. Why is it important for us to be able to share, one to one, with people who truly understand our painful situations?

5. What, according to Ephesians 5:22–24, is the woman's role?

6. Read Ephesians 5:25–33. What does it mean, in practical terms, for the husband to love his wife as Christ loves the church? As he loves himself?

7. Discuss each of the following four principles found in Genesis 2:24–25. If you feel comfortable doing so, discuss which one(s) you struggle with the most.

   ◄ Leave

   ◄ Cleave

   ◄ Become one flesh

   ◄ Naked and not ashamed

8. Why, if one spouse abdicates his or her biblical role, should the other spouse continue to obey the principles God set up?

CHAPTER 10

1. Why can't we depend on the church alone to protect us from ourselves?

2. What kinds of things make us vulnerable to sexual temptation? Why do we have to be so careful about the "small things" in our relationships with the opposite sex?

3. What are you doing to guard the "relational space" you share with your spouse? What does it mean to "flee" from sexual immorality? (See 1 Corinthians 6:18.)

4. Why do Internet chats, daydreaming about people other than our spouses, or "emotional" affairs often lead to sexual relationships? What "hedges" can we establish to protect our marriages, and why must we establish them *now*?

5. What is lust, and what does Jesus say about it in Matthew 5:28?

6. What are some ways in which a couple can rekindle their intimacy? Romance each other? Be accountable to one another?

7. Read Psalm 51 and consider the requests David made in this prayer after his affair with Bathsheba.

8. What stood out to you as you read Gary's letter at the end of the book? Why?

The Word at Work Around the World

A vital part of Cook Communications Ministries is our international outreach, Cook Communications Ministries International (CCMI). Your purchase of this book, and of other books and Christian-growth products from Cook, enables CCMI to provide Bibles and Christian literature to people in more than 150 languages in 65 countries.

Cook Communications Ministries is a not-for-profit, self-supporting organization. Revenues from sales of our books, Bible curricula, and other church and home products not only fund our U.S. ministry, but also fund our CCMI ministry around the world. One hundred percent of donations to CCMI go to our international literature programs.

CCMI reaches out internationally in three ways:

- Our premier International Christian Publishing Institute (ICPI) trains leaders from nationally led publishing houses around the world.

- We provide literature for pastors, evangelists, and Christian workers in their national language.

- We reach people at risk—refugees, AIDS victims, street children, and famine victims—with God's Word.

Word Power, God's Power

Faith Kidz, RiverOak, Honor, Life Journey, Victor, NexGen — every time you purchase a book produced by Cook Communications Ministries, you not only meet a vital personal need in your life or in the life of someone you love, but you're also a part of ministering to José in Colombia, Humberto in Chile, Gousa in India, or Lidiane in Brazil. You help make it possible for a pastor in China, a child in Peru, or a mother in West Africa to enjoy a life-changing book. And because you helped, children and adults around the world are learning God's Word and walking in his ways.

Thank you for your partnership in helping to disciple the world. May God bless you with the power of his Word in your life.

For more information about our international ministries, visit www.ccmi.org.